The Beautiful Days of My Youth

The Beautiful Days of My Youth

My Six Months in Auschwitz and Plaszow

Ana Novac

Translated from the French
by George L. Newman

Preface and notes by
Myrna Goldenberg, Ph.D.

Henry Holt and Company
New York

Henry Holt and Company, Inc.
Publishers since 1866
115 West 18th Street
New York, New York 10011

Henry Holt is a registered
trademark of Henry Holt and Company, Inc.

First published in the United States in 1997 by Henry Holt and Company, Inc.
Published in Canada by Fitzhenry & Whiteside Ltd.,
195 Allstate Parkway, Markham, Ontario L3R 4T8.
Originally published in France in 1992 by Editions Balland under the
title *Les Beaux Jours de ma jeunesse.*

Library of Congress Cataloging-in-Publication Data
Novac, Ana.
   [Beaux jours de ma jeunesse. English]
   The beautiful days of my youth: my six months in Auschwitz / by Ana
Novac; translated from the French by George L. Newman.
     p.   cm.
   1. Auschwitz (Concentration camp). 2. Novac, Ana. 3. Holocaust, Jewish
(1939–1945)—Personal narratives. I. Title.
   D805.P7Z8713   1996   940.53′ 18′092—dc21   [B]   96-49263

ISBN 0-8050-5018-3

First American Edition—1997
Designed by Debbie Glasserman

Jacket photo from the Central State Archive of the October Revolution,
Byelorussia, courtesy of the USHMM Photo Archives.

Map of Cracow-Plaszow, page 57, courtesy of the University Press of Florida.
Map on page 16 drawn by Jurgen Pieoplow, from *Auschwitz Chronicle, 1939–
1945,* by Danuta Czech, published by Henry Holt and Company, Inc., 1990.

Printed in the United States of America on acid-free paper. ∞

10 9 8 7 6 5 4 3 2 1

Unfamiliar terms that appear in the glossary are italicized when first used in
the text.

In memory of my family

Contents

Preface

A journal written in a concentration camp, where life itself is precarious and survival largely a matter of luck, is a rare artifact. When it is written by an observant, literary teenager, it is transformed into a rare treasure. Ana Novac's journal is such a treasure. It is an extraordinary work by a well-educated, sensitive fifteen-year-old Hungarian girl whose insights and talents were honed in Auschwitz and Plaszow in 1944. Her writing was a response to her intense passion to bear witness to the atrocities and daily terror of the concentration camp as perfected by the Nazis. She chronicles life in two of those camps, one of which has become a widely recognized symbol of atrocity, and the other, familiar through the motion picture *Schindler's List* as the site of Oskar Schindler's factory.

Stunning in its detail and imagery, Ana's portrayal of fellow prisoners and the hierarchy of prisoner-supervisors is a drama complete with scenes and a cast of characters. Through her witty caricatures, we meet prisoners up and down the chain of privilege, from the ordinary inmate like Ana herself to inmates who supervise barracks and work groups. Among them are Sophie, her closest friend; her unnamed benefactor, the sculptress; Madame Potrez, the pompous, self-important senior prisoner, "half monkey and half chicken," and her terrifying laugh; Jurek, the lonely, inscrutable brutal whip-cracking sentry, who sometimes uses a snake in place of a whip; sleepy, lazy Konhauser, the head of the clothing depot, who recognizes her spunk after he loses his; exuberant, tall, bald, S-shaped Juliette whose antics send the inmates into gales of laughter during disinfection; and even the red-faced, mean, criminal Goliath-like Kapo Otto. Our view of the camp Commandant, Amon Goeth, the "panting whale," the sadistic brute astride his white horse, is unusual; we see him from her hiding place as he virtually gallops over her.

She shows us the barracks, the quarries, the *Appelplatz*, the latrines, and the work sites. We work, march, starve and eat, stand motionless for hours at roll call, feel the pain of the blows she gets, and cry with her. And we fear with her and for her as she writes in secluded spaces, in her bunk while she should be sleeping, in sight of the barracks seniors, and in secret when discovery could mean severe punishment or worse. Indeed, her journal vibrates with people and places, shouted orders and intimate conversation, hope and despair, and humor and tears. It also vibrates with her courage.

Some of her courage stems from the relationships with other women. They form surrogate or substitute families that fill some of the loneliness that comes from being torn from family and friends. Sophie, a friend from home who finds her in the crowd of naked, bald women, is her closest companion and although they sometimes irritate each other, more often they comfort and protect each other. Sophie sometimes grumbles about Ana's preoccupation with her journal, but she helps Ana hide it. She knows its value, both to Ana and to the world outside the barbed wire fences of the concentration camp. Ana is thoroughly annoyed at Sophie's philosophizing and intellectual approach to everything, but, as she watches her sleep, Ana is compassionate and writes that Sophie is "just a poor kid, exhausted and dirty. She's holding her arm folded over her bald head as if to protect it." Ana begs a Kapo to include Sophie in her clothing work group. "My best friend, please, take her in the group," she pleads unsuccessfully. Another prisoner, the sculptress "adopts" Ana and finishes her quota of hard labor just as Ana is about to drop from exhaustion. She shelters her during the three-day cattle car trip from Plaszow to Auschwitz. Together, they form the "council of three" as a strategy of survival.

Ana's portraits of these small groupings reinforces the comments of other survivor writers who tell us that these surrogate families contributed significantly to their survival and that being alone in the concentration camp diminished one's chances of surviving. Charlotte Delbo[1] and Sara Nomberg-Przytyk,[2] in their twenties when they were sent to Auschwitz, each insist that caring for others and being cared about saved them from surrendering to loneliness and despair. When Isabella Leitner[3] advises her readers that "to be sisterless" means that a prisoner "did not have the pressure, the absolute responsibility to end the day alive," she is pointing to the necessity of forming family-type groups, of becoming someone's "camp sister." "Camp sisters" accepted responsibility for each other's survival, including sharing food, risking punishments, and encouraging each other in the face of hopelessness. Ana and Sophie were "camp sis-

---

[1] Charlotte Delbo, a member of the French Resistance and a survivor of Auschwitz, is the author of the trilogy *Auschwitz and After* (Yale University Press, 1995).

[2] Sara Nomberg-Przytyk, also an Auschwitz survivor, has written *Auschwitz: True Tales from a Grotesque Land,* translated by Roslyn Hirsch (University of North Carolina Press, 1985).

[3] All quotations from Isabella Leitner come from her memoir *The Big Lie: A True Story of Isabella Leitner* (with Irving A. Leitner; illustrated by Judy Pedersen; Scholastic, 1992).

ters." For a short while, the sculptress was Ana's "camp mother." Not all the prisoners in this journal are likeable or helpful, nor do they all devote themselves to the well-being of someone else. Ana draws them all, without sentiment or sympathy.

Ana's journal has several dimensions. Not only is it a testimony with strong historical value, but, like Anne Frank's diary, it is also a delicate unfolding of an adolescent's development as a writer. Robbed of a normal life of schooling and parties and all the joys and crises of a bright teenager, Ana, a prisoner in a concentration camp, feels the hopelessness of her situation and weeps in despair. A witness to unspeakable violence and unimaginable living conditions, she desperately seeks solace. She finds it in her journal. Her journal writing is her method of protecting her memory, which is what distinguishes her from everyone else and the only part of herself that she is not required to share. To retain her memory, she forces herself to recall trivia, for example, the names of elementary school classmates. Her journal, she declares, "was what allowed me to survive."

In the face of the Nazi machine that was created to degrade, exploit, and finally annihilate her, she struggles to invent ways to affirm her worth and to defy her enemies. Her writing becomes her tool for survival, a way to prevent effacement by the enemy. It is, she says, her "second [skin] . . . what keeps the rest from falling apart." The writing process is proof that she exists as "somebody": "I'm alive! I'm writing . . . choosing my words, 'composing.' " Thus, her journal is practical as well as spiritual. Because it gives her purpose, it also gives her the will and the strength to stay alive.

"If you were a racehorse, I'd bet on you," a Kapo tells her, revealing his admiration and even awe for her courageous journal keeping. As the close and relentless observer, Ana is the keeper of accounts whose words will indict her jailers. Motivated to write and record the events of the camps, scene by scene, Ana resists surrendering to the starvation, slave labor, violence, and suffering. The very act of writing emboldens her to fight her weariness and hunger and to stand as a counterforce to the Nazis. She refuses to become invisible and her journal is her weapon against the powerful, elaborate system of the Third Reich. The journal is more than an artifact of life in the camps. It is an artifact of resistance. Thus, we are invited to revise the familiar saying that the pen is mightier than the sword. In Ana's case, it is the only possible alternative to the sword.

Ana's journal is also a strong source of wisdom and wit, laced with grim ironic camp humor that is seldom present in books about the Holocaust. Ana comes to understand what politicians and statesmen too often ignore: the "difference between a full belly and an empty belly is perhaps the greatest difference that there has ever been on earth." When she becomes philosophical, Sophie reminds her of the absurdity of the concentration camp by telling her that she has a "dangerous tendency to relapse into logic." Her comments on Sophie reveal wit beyond the insight of most fifteen-year-olds: Sophie "inhabits her body like a bachelor in a furnished room: She doesn't love it, but she isn't particularly embarrassed by it; she's not that interested in it." The barracks supervisor reminds Ana of a pitiful classmate, the kind of girl whose "garter belt came unhooked just at the moment when she was called up to the blackboard."

Ana adds to the concentration camp lexicon. Vitamin J, or news about the war, is the Jewish vitamin. "Angel-makers" are abortionists. The "market" is the animated bazaar where the trick is "to get rid of a piece of merchandise that nobody needs, at a price [usually bread] that you yourself think is scandalous." The latrine in Auschwitz is the "club," international but not cosmopolitan. She and Sophie declare themselves "masons" when asked to identify their "professions." What's more "marvelous," romanticizes Sophie, "than a body with muscles taut from working." They are assigned to the quarry, along with everyone else, including those who declared themselves "society woman" or "cook." After a few days of hard labor and punishing blows, Ana learns an important lesson: "Avoid *nature* as well as the Fritzes when you're 'concentrated.'" The huge wooden shoes she is issued in Auschwitz are the source of hilarity. Fellow prisoners assure her that "once the mud freezes," she'll be able to take up "cross-country skiing and other winter sports." Perhaps crazy laughter is the prisoners' only possible response to their misery because "tears are the first thing to dry up."

Ana Novac's journal is a rich, unforgettable account of the most brutalizing, murderous setting in recorded history. Unpretentious, vivid, informative, honest, and beautifully—often poetically—written, it is indeed a rare treasure.

As Zimra Harsanyi, the name she used at Auschwitz, she began a literary career that did not end with liberation. As Ana Novac, she has been a very successful playwright and novelist. After recuperating from the camps, she studied theater and psychology in Bucharest, where her first plays were produced. Her work was also staged in Hungary and the former Soviet Union. By the mid-sixties, she had moved to Berlin and wrote radio dramas for German radio. From 1968 to 1972, she saw some of her plays produced in Paris, where she has lived since 1970. Novac turned to writing novels. Her most recent works, *Un lit dans l'Hexagone* (1993) and *Les Noces de Varenka* (1996), have earned praise for their force, brilliance, and irony, the same qualities that characterize her first work, *The Beautiful Days of My Youth.*

MYRNA GOLDENBERG

Dr. Myrna Goldenberg, a scholar on the experiences of women during the holocaust, teaches undergraduate Holocaust studies at Montgomery College outside Washington, D.C., and graduate courses at the Johns Hopkins University in Baltimore. In 1996 she won the national annual William H. Meardy Outstanding Faculty Award.

The Beautiful Days of My Youth

Ana Novac shortly after the war

Introduction

I was born in Transylvania, a region that three peoples—Romanian, Hungarian, and German—have argued over in three languages for centuries. That is why, except for an accident of birth (the fact that I am Jewish) I have never been able to specify precisely either my nationality or my native language. I came into the world under a fascist dictatorship, spent my youth under a communist dictatorship, and between the two, for a change of pace, I did a tour at Auschwitz and seven other concentration camps.

When I was born, on June 21, 1929, at Dej, in northern Transylvania, that town was Romanian. At the beginning of the war, the part of Transylvania where we lived became Hungarian once again, then Romanian again after the war. In three generations my family changed nationality four times.

My maiden name was Zimra Harsanyi. My father, Eugen Harsanyi, was an attorney in a town that started out being called Grossvardein in German, then Nagyvarad in Hungarian, and then Oradea-Mare in Romanian. He was a defense lawyer known and detested by all the regimes, disbarred even before the introduction of the racial laws. He was renowned for his "annoying" habit of defending lost causes, keeping (or getting) politically "inconvenient" people out of prison: militant Catholics (in an Orthodox country), Freemasons, Communists, and anarchists of every sort. He never personally "suffered" from any ideology, being as far from Communism or Freemasonry as he was from Catholicism. (I think that I inherited from him my extreme distrust of all ideologies.) Yet he had a belief for which he struggled his entire life: Any idea that is restricted or persecuted may become a fad, a collective obsession, and even fanaticism, which is the greatest danger to the human spirit.

My mother, born Margarethe Ehrenfeld, was originally from Germany. Her father, a rabbi in Bremen, had the good fortune to die before Hitler came to power; it was a good fortune that no member of his family was to share. His four sons were deported from Germany and my mother from Hungary, along with my father, my brother, and all the other members of our tribe (some forty people)—to whom I would add my fellow students at the Jewish high school in Miskolc.

Given the causes that my father defended, and the precarious situation of his clients, our life was not easy. As far as I can remember (until the Nazis put an end to all our worries), the *rent* always hovered over our heads like a sinister cloud. Process servers haunted the house, bills were overdue, and so on. Strangely, none of this ever undermined my parents' ironic sense of humor, their superb detachment, or their generosity. For my brother and me they were princes, beings of light, who could never be either humiliated or embittered by the sordid details of our situation.

At the age of eleven, because of a long illness—a case of double pleurisy—I lived for more than a year on a chaise-longue, taking the air of the Carpathians. It was there that I began keeping my journal, which I continued at Auschwitz and preserved until the Liberation.

I started school in Romanian and continued in Hungarian; then, expelled from the Hungarian state school, I went temporarily to the Jewish high school in Miskolc, a Hungarian town. I was in Miskolc when suddenly, in the course of a single night, the Fritzes invaded Hungary (in the spring of 1944). It was the last year of the war, when the Allied victory was no longer in doubt.

After I went to Miskolc, I never saw either my parents or my brother again. I know that they were waiting for my return, to try to flee to the part of Transylvania that the Nazis had left to the Romanians (who were not deporting people at the time)—except that I was arrested and taken off the train after a check of identity papers. Only my baggage arrived in Oradea, and my parents gave up the attempt to flee; I was thus, in spite of myself, the cause of their deportation and death.

There were a number of us (dozens, hundreds?) who were taken off the train, shut up in a synagogue, and threatened with being burned alive along with the synagogue, if the Jewish community refused to pay a sum of money—the amount of which escapes me. The community must have paid the money, because we got out alive and were transferred to the ghetto, on the site of a brickyard.

In the ghetto there was a rush to suicide, a veritable epidemic, which was reserved for the *rich*, because the cyanide that people brought in—God knows how—commanded phenomenal prices. To die before being piled up in the railroad cars was the supreme luxury, but one to which only the privileged could aspire. I was alone, with no money, no luggage, no cyanide; and no way to get fed, because the majority of those who were unsuccessful in their pursuit of death had to feed their own families.

I made several escape attempts, all failures; in my

rundown condition, starving and in rags, I was spotted at once (usually by kids my age), and invariably brought back to the brickyard. It was after my last escape attempt, when I saw the place thick with people, that I calmed myself by saying, "Whatever happens to them will happen to me."

After that I was a zombie. It was the best thing that could have happened to me: total apathy about my life and death. Stricken by a benign amnesia, rescued from my memory, I no longer have any idea about the railroad cars, our trip, or our arrival at Auschwitz. My first memory is of a pencil stub that I found in the sand, which (since I had spent the past three years keeping a journal, and living only for that journal) seemed to me to be a sign, a "suggestion" from fate.

From that moment on, my story was the story of my journal, which covers the period from June to November, 1944.

How can one write under conditions where existing, simply breathing, was a moment-to-moment miracle? A pencil stub . . . camouflage paper (gray, fortunately) . . . posters saying WORK WILL MAKE YOU FREE, CLEANLINESS IS HEALTH, and other things, which I pulled off walls and cut up to make sheets. Shoes—the only thing they returned to us after the "disinfections"—served to hide the pages. When too many accumulated, I learned them by heart and summed up each chapter in a few words, which I would use to reconstruct the journal once I arrived at a new camp. It involved risks, of course, but they were not as great as I feared. In reality the Germans were not very concerned about the subversive ideas that might be held by "thinkers" who were destined to be snuffed out before long: The new technique (the gas chambers) allowed massive, rapid, and inexpensive executions.

Of the eight camps I passed through, I remember only the ones that appear in my journal, during the time when I still had the energy to write. Was it the end of May, or was it June when I arrived at Auschwitz? Was I in Camp B or C? Did I stay for three weeks, or more? After that came the camp at Plaszow (a suburb of Cracow, so they said). Was I at Plaszow for six weeks, or more? My second stay at Auschwitz, to judge from the heat, must have been in late July or August.

The thing I'm nearly certain of is that I arrived at Wiesau in September. I deduce that from the color of the trees: red. By the end of October, or November, I was in the hospital with my pleurisy in relapse; the final pages of the journal were written there. From then until my liberation, my only concern was to hide those pages in my shoes or the shoes of companions who were willing to help.

I remember a long march in the snow. Did it last for

days, or weeks? I remember it because of the hunger: There was no more bread or soup. We weren't allowed to look for grass or leaves for "nourishment," or to pick up those who fell, or we would get a bullet in the back.

After that came two or three more camps, about which I haven't the slightest idea. The last was in Czechoslovakia, at Kratzau, where we were liberated on May 6, 1945, by the Tartars.

In the camps, my first concerns were finding paper and arranging to get the top sleeping platform, in order to take advantage of the dim, greenish light from the ceiling, which never went out and which allowed me to work on my journal at night. Today I am convinced that the journal was what allowed me to survive. For the rest of my life, it has also been a way to survive that *survival,* which is a less obvious problem. The fact that I had the toughness to live, to function, to keep my health and my sanity, after and despite the loss of my family, meant that—as illogical as it may seem—I carried, and still carry, the weight of a solitary crime: having lived. Absurd, you say; but it has never been erased from my conscience, and never pardoned by it.

My parents died of typhus shortly after the Liberation, and my brother—younger than I—was apparently a victim of the gas.

I don't remember how or by whom I was repatriated to Cluj (in Transylvania, which was once again Romanian), to a Jewish hospital where I spent two years on my deathbed—to judge by the behavior of the people around me—but perfectly conscious. I weighed seventy-five pounds and had close to a dozen ailments, each of them life-threatening.

I was struck with a lasting amnesia that continued after my release from the hospital and allowed me to live out my youth, complete my education—at the Theater Institute and at the university, where I studied psychology—and become an actress and then a playwright. All I knew about the camp was that I had been there, that my family had remained there, and that I had made notes there, which I had brought back with me and put away somewhere.

When sixteen years later, in the course of moving, I came across a large bundle of handwritten pages, I at first wondered what they were. As luck would have it my eye fell on a legible passage that I found "funny." I relived the camp during the time that I spent deciphering my impossible writing. I worked for several months with a magnifying glass to prepare a text in Hungarian, as faithful to the manuscript as possible.

That text was rejected by the censors as "anti-Semitic" at a time when my career as a dramatic author was at its height, with my plays performed nearly everywhere behind the Iron Curtain. It's useless to explain to a bureaucrat trembling for his job and his life that one can be Jewish, persecuted, and a bastard at the same time; that martyrdom and heroism do not necessarily go together; that misfortune does not imply any merit and does not confer any more right to glory than a car wreck or an earthquake. Useless, in short, to explain and reexplain that I neither invented, added, nor falsified anything, disdaining any form of compromise with respect to myself, my people, our allies, or our saviors.

In 1963 I left my country after undergoing a witch trial as a "subversive element" and being expelled from the Writers' Union. I managed to get the typed copy of my notes out across several socialist borders. It was that copy that my collaborator—the poet Jean Parvulesco—and I used to make the French translation published by Julliard in 1968. As successive editions appeared I refused to reexamine that translation, saying only, "Think of me as having died." The truth is that I had an aversion to the subject, which I finally conquered recently when the question of an American edition came up.

I reread the text. What had seemed acceptable to me, with my French of thirty years before, gave me an unpleasant surprise. It was the work of a diligent scholar: flat, without rhythm, sticking timidly to the words at the expense of meaning and style. I had a

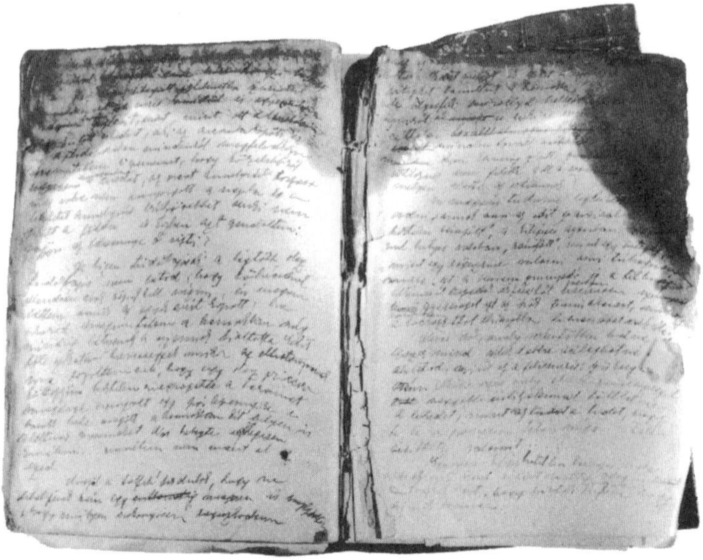

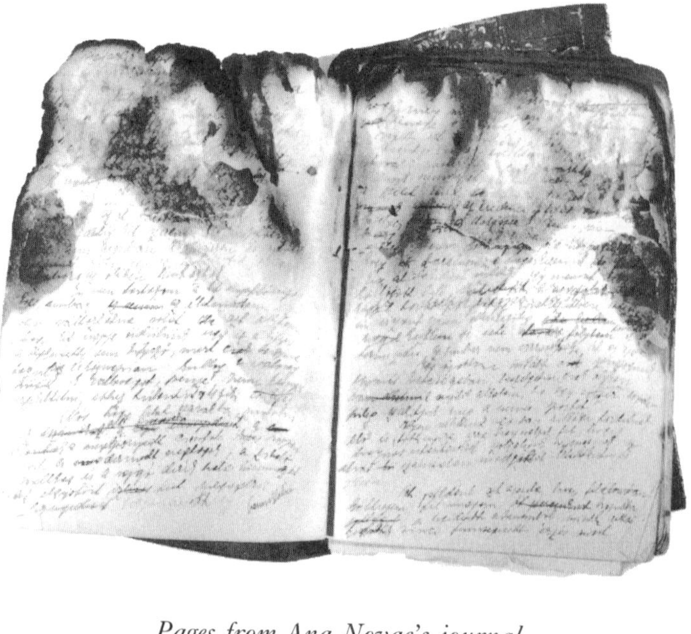

Pages from Ana Novac's journal

e: rework the existing translation to make it less clumsy and less labored, or simply *awaken* the text and bring it back to life in the French that is now my language as much as Hungarian once was. Since the typed Hungarian copy was nowhere to be found, apparently lost in the course of my wanderings and my innumerable moves, I went back to the original manuscript—the condition of which you can imagine, after half a century! I scoured Paris, trying out different magnifying glasses. Thanks to a good friend, I had the opportunity to work for a few hours a day in a lab, using precision equipment, and I was thus able to reconstruct certain passages that were illegible using the magnifying glasses of my youth. I eliminated certain fragments—verbose, trivial, or boring—that weighed down the rhythm. I made very few changes to the content, but rather to the style, tone, and music of the French. I may not have been able to achieve the brevity and the wonderful flexibility of Hungarian, but I think I approached it as smoothly as possible.

People have commented that my journal is surprisingly "mature," considering my age at the time I wrote it. I can say in all honesty that I did not "doctor" my account, or impose on it a false maturity. I simply gave back to it, in a different language, its original punch, impudence, and freedom. The "maturity" of my journal is the natural result of long patience and profound solitude, which I would never have experienced without the immobility and silence imposed by the pleurisy that I contracted at the age of eleven.

I believe that this new French version (on which the English translation is based) is the closest to my original text. It is all the more important to me because this sorrowful chapter of history, which I wanted only to strike from my memory, seems after half a century to be ineradicable and, alas, of a more and more dreadful timeliness.

The Journal

What could I have written on this page? I don't know. And on the one before? It's all obliterated. The paper is a faded scrap, devoured by time. From what tomb of memory have they escaped, these drunken letters? Memory? No, the thread that leads there has been cut for a long time. The memory of something that long ago I must surely have remembered, something real and vivid that happened to me but that merciful forgetfulness has pushed farther and farther away, and that continues to grow more and more faint, like those stories that we sometimes tell out of habit but that no longer concern us. It's a stranger who deciphers these ancient pages. Her uneasiness and her astonishment are ancient.

I'm only recopying. After two torn, illegible pages comes a sentence that begins (or continues) like this:

———

"You're gonna die," hisses the Slovak, with a nasty laugh. This girl, who is usually so impassive, rouses

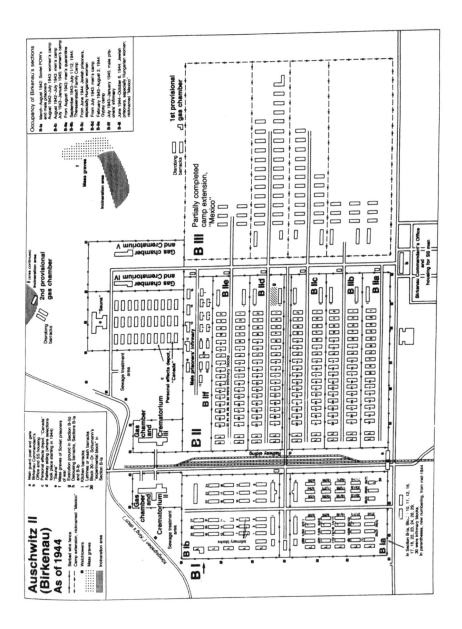

Auschwitz II (Birkenau) As of 1944

- ■ Barbed wire fence
- ---- Camp extension, nicknamed "Mexico"
- ● Watchtowers
- Mass graves
- :::: Incineration area

- a Main guard post and gate
- b Birkenau Commandant's Office and SS housing
- c Personal effects depot, "Canada"
- d Railway siding (where selections took place starting in 1944)
- f "Sauna"
- g Mass graves of Soviet prisoners
- g Execution ground in Section B-IId
- h Delousing barracks, Sections B-Ia and B-Ib
- i Kitchen barracks
- L Latrine and wash barracks
- 30 Block 30—Dr. Schumann's "experimental block" in Section B-Ia

In Section B-Ia, Blocks 10, 11, 12, 16, 17, 18, 22, 23, 24, 28, 29, 30 were infirmary blocks.
In parentheses, new numbering, from mid-1944

Occupancy of Birkenau's sections

- B-Ia March–August 1942: Soviet POW's and male prisoners
  August 1942–July 1943: women's camp
- B-Ib August 1942–July 1943: men's camp
  July 1943–January 1945: women's camp
- B-IIa From August 1943: men's quarantine
- B-IIb September 1943–July 11/12, 1944: Theresienstadt Family Camp
- B-IIc From June 1944: Jewish prisoners, especially Hungarian women
- B-IId From July 1943: men's camp
- B-IIe February 1943–August 2, 1944: Gypsy camp
- B-IIf July 1943–January 1945: male prisoners' infirmary
- B-III June 1944–October 6, 1944: Jewish prisoners, especially Hungarian women; nicknamed "Mexico"

1st provisional gas chamber

Disrobing barracks

Partially completed camp extension, "Mexico"

B III

Disrobing barracks

2nd provisional gas chamber

Incineration area (area continues)

Mass graves

Incineration area

Gas chamber and Crematorium V

Gas chamber and Crematorium IV

"Sauna"

Sewage treatment area

Personal effects depot, "Canada"

Male prisoners' infirmary

B IIf
B IIe
B IId
B IIc
B IIb
B IIa

B II

Gas chamber and Crematorium III

Railway siding

Birkenau Commandant's Office and housing for SS men

Sewage treatment area

Königsweg ("King's Way")

Gas chamber and Crematorium II

B Ib

B Ia

B I

Infirmary blocks

herself only to hit. It revives her, like a tennis player who after long, tedious training finally throws herself into the match. Her chin juts out and her beautiful indolent lips, pressed tightly together, are only a line. For a moment she watches her prey, her eyes narrowed, motionless. Then her mouth brightens with a half smile that's a little dreamy, or playful. The whip draws back, the better to strike with its full force. A series of delicious sensations on this face that is otherwise unexpressive.

The Slovak had been standing polite and still, behind the Germans. Doll Face chuckled. Her shrill voice wounded the night silence. She turned and said something to the Slovak, who acknowledged the order and started running along the ranks, through the gate, and out the main entrance. The darkness soon swallowed the retreating blond form.

"Where have they sent her? To do what?"

This isn't the first night that we've spent like this, standing in ranks of five, not knowing what we're waiting for or what we're afraid of. My feet swell, my chest tightens. Anxiety . . . I feel it growing in my body, a fat beast, dark and sticky.

The minutes pass, and then we hear the Slovak's voice across the barbed wire: "Links, links, links, und links."[1] The newcomers are many, it seems—a thou-

---

[1] Left, left, left, and left.

sand or more. A murmur runs through and agitates the ranks. How did they find out? It's a mystery, but everyone knows: The neighboring camp is being evacuated. This huge *transport* will be housed with us. We watch them approach: a thousand empty bellies, a thousand bunks. Our wary looks meet haggard eyes. These women are even more run down and skinny than we are. They must have been at Auschwitz longer; they're in rags.

After a few seconds the camp telegraph (communicating the maximum amount of information with a minimum of gestures and no sound at all) is connected.

"Where are you from?" I ask a girl who stops for a moment in front of me. "Oradea," she whispers, and her hunted expression seems familiar to me, even in the uncertain light of the street lamps. Perhaps it's because of the name of the town—my town. They've already started moving again. The drooping shoulders, the slightly rolling walk . . . Judy! My lips move but my throat is dry. Not a sound comes out. My eyes are riveted on the familiar back: "Turn around! Turn around! Turn around!" I look at her with all my strength, all my willpower. A miracle. She stops. She doesn't recognize me, her eyes pass over me, indifferent. But after a few steps she freezes and turns around, stunned—my face, which she has just brushed with a distracted look, must have taken shape in her mind. These awful rags! She cries out in an incomprehensible, unfamiliar voice: my name, perhaps. Emotion makes me deaf. I no longer see her— only the rhythmic movement of the Slovak's back, and right next to my shoulder, the whip that she's brandishing. It's Judy that she's hitting.

I don't move. I watch the back bend and straighten, as if everything depended on my following the slightest movement.

"What's happening?" asks someone in the last rank.

"She's attending to the new ones."

Not a head turns.

"You have to get used to it," I say to myself, "not be anything or anyone, just a shadow with a useless memory, one in a rank of five, *one fifth*."

If, in a moment of madness, I cried out, "I am So-and-so. The one being whipped is my friend, the president of the literary society at school, a strong personality, an excitable little thing"—if I started barking like a dog, without a doubt it wouldn't cause any greater hilarity. There are times when revealing your thoughts, the tiniest part of yourself, is so out of place that it verges on the ridiculous. That's why we all live shut up in our cocoons. The rank of five is the cage and the cloak. The number is our disguise. A meeting of masks. The human cowering behind does her best to hide what she once took delight in flaunting: her soul. That's how the hard and merciful armor is forged.

—

A nightmare: I had misplaced my pencil. I woke up terrified, and heedless of the gasping and the snores, I started rummaging in my straw mattress. My pencil was in its place. Now I'm writing. I'm writing that I'm writing. Praise the Lord or the luck, it hardly matters which, that let my feet, among so many feet, so many steps, stumble over it. But did I really stumble? Or did I simply stop beside a thing that wouldn't have attracted anyone's attention, any more than a crushed cigarette butt? I stopped at that moment, in that place. This chewed-up thing, plucked from the mud, gives back to me at every moment, in secret, what an entire world of madmen is trying to take away from me: the joy of saying "Shit!"

—

I saw Judy. Just for a second, but beyond a doubt. Our eyes met one time. Just one time. We both turned away, and as if by an unspoken agreement, we never looked for each other after that.

The circle of naked bodies, under the red sky, and all these moving shadows . . . like something out of another time, or a savage tale. The elegant figure at the center—the chief of the tribe? Only his uniform seems out of place. It strikes a false note. He's whistling; with a repetitive motion of his thumb, he makes a body leave the circle every few moments. His finger moves in rhythm, and the circle tightens at the same cadence. We turn faster and faster . . . fewer and fewer of us. What for? (Another question. Won't I ever break that habit?) The Germans are teaching us to dance.

Bizarre! During this ritual I didn't ask myself any questions. Nothing surprised me. I moved, I circled, weightlessly, effortlessly, as if in a dream.

But that's not what I wanted to talk about. Judy! When it was over I stopped, reeling, and then I saw the line of naked bodies leaving and anxiety sobered me up; as if through indiscretion or cowardice I had done something irreparable. I ran back and forth in the darkness, calling her name. She was not among the ones who remained. That was when Sophie found me.

She took me by the arm with a forcefulness that was unusual for her. (I laugh now when I think about it. What could be more grotesque than two bald, naked people clinging to each other!)

"Lucky they took them away," she said. "There'll be more room in the barracks."

I kept quiet; I would have very much preferred that she had been the one they took away, and Judy who had stayed.

—

Impossible to get to sleep. Fortunately the barracks is never completely dark; you can write. But how will I decipher these hieroglyphics? No matter! If only I can shake off this burden of crushing thoughts. Get rid of them. In truth I protect myself from that burden—I jump over certain of my thoughts as if they were bottomless holes—whereas perhaps all I need to do is let myself be sucked into that thick depression. And there, in the depths where I can sink no farther, to sleep at last, empty of anguish and of dreams. But from here to there is a long way, I know. And there is this endless night, and Judy, and the all-pervading question: Why did she have to show up, only to disappear at once? These past two days: two times twenty-four hours wasted. Why didn't we look for each other? And at the end that cowardly, shameful good-bye! Were we embarrassed by our nakedness? No, it wasn't just that. There are quiet, patient friendships, for rainy days. Ours was uneasy, impetuous like Judy, timid and intense like me. And like both of us, it was very changeable.

Why put the things you care about to the *test?* Scratching and coughing together, enduring the smells and the fears while holding each other by the hand? Why tamper with fragile images? Why not keep the image of Judy as she was: plump, soft, extravagant, full of whimsy and impulsiveness! Rich! She claimed she didn't care and that was true, except that impulsiveness rarely emerges from a basement flat. She'd say, "We'll do this, we'll go there," without adding, "If you want to." I'd answer "No" with a light tone and a heavy heart.

Those pangs of pride! How many others have I known since then! But those old, childhood sorrows, I try to preserve them because they're the only ones I don't share with my rank of five.

—

Girls younger than sixteen are supposed to come forward. It was just announced at roll call; they'll go to another camp, where the old people and children are waiting for them. Excellent conditions: bread and butter in the morning, individual beds, blankets, clean plates, and baths every day. According to the rumors, that camp is a place of rest, a kind of sanitorium; on lawns in the shade of big trees, the old people take their grandchildren for walks. Fantasies? Someone saw it. Stay calm. Here, someone has always seen everything (with her own eyes), and there's always someone to swear to it. Someone already *saw* the white bread, the new clothes waiting for us, and the toothbrushes; someone *saw* civilians, diplomats surely, negotiating in English with the SS on the *Lagerstrasse*. Others swear that this circus won't last more than a week. The circus is still going on, and in our ranks they continue tirelessly to "see" and to "swear." And who would argue about the white bread or the English diplomat, since "someone" saw the tub of jam that they're going to distribute, "someone" spotted American parachutes over the camp, and "someone" swore that it was true?

In our extreme deprivation, aren't we like the child alone in the dark, who jumps at every shadow and sees angels and devils dancing on the walls? One thing is certain: There are no children here, in this camp. No old people either. They must be somewhere. So why shouldn't they be together? Milk, bread and butter, individual beds—foolishness. But if it's only one percent true: that they're alive . . .

—

Enlightening conversation with Hella.

Today, during the cleaning, she caught me in bed. As usual, after roll call I had slipped back in for the only break in this scorching hell, a half hour of quiet. In principle the barracks is off limits during the cleaning, but I almost always manage to sneak in. She came up without a sound. When I noticed her, she must have been watching me for a while already.

"What are you doing there?"

"Scribbling."

"What?"

"Things."

She didn't say anything. She didn't have her stick. She could have used her fists, but maybe she was lazy—or was she disconcerted by the unexpected situation?

"Your paper, where did you get it?"

"I found it."

Suppose I had told her that I took it off the wall of the toilets, and that it said "Sauberkeit Ist Gesundheit"[1] on the back? But she didn't insist. She's not in form today. She asked me almost gently:

"Do you care about your skin?"

"A little."

"Then tear it up. Wegschmeissen!"[2]

She didn't even chase me out of my bunk.

Wegschmeissen! A funny situation. You know, Hella, I have two skins, and the second one—my notes—may be what keeps the rest from falling apart.

—

I'm hungry. Today all my thoughts take the shape of sausages . . . lethargy . . . I'm not worrying my brain anymore.

[1] Cleanliness Is Health.
[2] Throw it away!

—

They're searching feverishly for girls under sixteen. I persuaded Sophie that we should come forward. It's not just the hunger, although that's something. The nights are unbearable.

And then who knows, we might find one of our people. Today at roll call we stepped out of the ranks. Hella saw me. She grabbed me by the arm and pushed me back.

"Idiots," she whispered. "Come on, back in line!"

Without a word we went back to our places. It may have been stupid. Sophie's right; she's jealous. The Slovaks, at least the ones that have survived (the brutes), have been here for six years. They can't forgive us, the Hungarians, for the fact that we were eating bread and butter while they and theirs . . . And yet at that moment Hella didn't think! She didn't have time. Hella! What can I say about her? Neither human nor Nazi . . . Hella is the camp.

They talk a lot about "hostages," and Sophie talks to me about it all day long:

"Now that the outcome of the war is no longer in doubt, we are a valuable asset. Each of us is supposed to be exchanged for a German prisoner of war. Otherwise what would stop them from liquidating us on the spot, like they did with the Polish and Czech and German transports? Even under these subhuman conditions, the camp is costing millions. Why watch us and count us so relentlessly?"

It's obvious.

In Hella's look there was something that resembled fright. Two things that obvious in one head keep anything else out. That's enough. To sleep . . . and wake up somewhere else, anywhere else . . . in Latin composition class.

—

Something's pressing on the back of my neck, or on my cerebellum. The cerebellum is the center of what? I'll have to ask Sophie. Of memory, perhaps? Last night I wasn't able to remember which of the two is bigger, the earth or the moon. This morbid need to constantly examine myself, quiz myself! Some nights I'm not able to go to sleep until I've remembered the names of the girls who sat beside me in the fifth grade, or the date of the coronation of Andrew II of Hungary. A lack of vitamins? "Civilian" foolishness. Here there's only one master: fact. I'm only a scribe in its service. Any thought that doesn't obey that rule is just in the way.

This morning they were again looking for girls under sixteen. Doll Face grabbed one out of the ranks. She did look very young, twelve or so. She stared wide-eyed at the German; she didn't understand what they wanted from her. An older woman held on to her, probably her mother since nothing, neither a threat nor a slap, could make her let go. She clutched the child to her and babbled, "Sie bleibt da, meine Tochter."[1] Doll Face finally had had enough and gave her a kick in the ribs, and she collapsed with a groan. The German dragged the child away; the little girl followed her for a few steps, silent and docile, almost indifferent. Then she suddenly stopped and turned around, and before anyone could stop her, she ran to her mother, threw herself onto her, and clung there; her skinny body shook with dry sobs and a kind of hiccups.

"Sie ist hysterisch, die Kleine,"[2] said Doll Face, who still didn't intervene; she watched them, her short upper lip curling back even more, with the curiosity of a child watching the unexpected behavior of another child or an animal.

The convulsive embrace continued. We all waited, frozen, for something to happen.

Finally the German moved, approached the pair unhurriedly, and stopped a few paces away. The mother noticed her, let go of her daughter, and started to drag herself to her feet. Her lips moved and she

---

[1] She's staying here, she's my daughter.
[2] The little girl is hysterical.

opened her mouth, but she couldn't get any sound to come out. I've never seen anyone drown, but it must be like that.

I could see the German only in profile. A peaceful profile, childlike and satiated. That's why I didn't understand what happened, where the sudden shot came from. The kneeling figure took a peculiar tumble in the dust, and I asked the woman next to me:

"Did she faint?"

"Idiot!" she answered.

Doll Face slipped an object into her pocket that I hadn't seen her pull out, and it seemed to sparkle for a second in her hand—like a cigarette case. Then she ordered: *"Blocksperre!"* She passed in front of the wall of people, making a little jump to avoid the form stretched out on the ground with its bare legs spread—a broken puppet—and the child curled on it like a hump.

They herded us into the barracks.

—

All day long, Blocksperre. The barracks is a morgue. We're perched on the upper bunk. Sophie is "philosophizing." I'm cutting up camouflage paper. One side is lighter, good enough for my notes. I already have a whole pile of it on the bunk, and all at once I'm stopped short by these questions: Am I all right? Did I really see that sort of hump in the burning sun this morning? Do I have heatstroke, am I delirious?

I just remembered: I've forgotten to introduce Sophie. Well, she's short, stocky, covered with freckles, and what she used to have that was nice, her red curls, now frame her homely face in the form of a sparse down. She inhabits her body like a bachelor in a furnished room: She doesn't love it, but she isn't particularly embarrassed by it; she's not that interested in it. There are so many other things to be interested in! Sophie claims to be a free spirit. If there's one thing she's proud of, it's her *detachment.*

Our friendship, too, is detached, as if we were communicating at a great distance through an alien medium. Her domain is theory; I don't have a "domain," except for feelings that change constantly, pulling me the way powerful horses pull an empty carriage. I'm afraid of maturity, a "role" that I'm not sure I'll be able to assume, while Sophie seems not to have kept any of her childishness. Maybe she was born this way, mature, thoughtful, and neutral like the angels; she acts like she understood everything and accomplished everything while she was still in diapers. "So what? What does it matter! Doesn't everything bring us closer to the final solution?"

The final solution! I've noticed it before: Sophie avoids referring to death by name, but she talks about it a lot and becomes strangely animated. Sometimes

I'm tempted to ask what's stopping her, since all it would take is to touch the electrified barbed wire: One second and it's over.

Maybe she's less afraid of dying than of being deprived of her "dissertations." Those blasted "analyses"—on education, for example, which from the cradle instills panic and keeps us from accepting the end as "naturally" as we do the beginning, from withdrawing without a fuss.

Hell! Did she see that woman's face when the German took aim? It wasn't "educated."

Will she ever be able to understand that she's wasting her intellect? Because I'm entirely of this world, and there's no philosophy, humiliation, misery, or pain that can extinguish my desire to live, however absurd that may be. And whether I'm writing or talking, I see only that face—its freckles, its beads of sweat—and it's as if her death rattle was coming from my own lungs . . .

All I want is to weep or pray, but not in front of a thinking machine! She irritates me and I end up finding an excellent reason to get mad.

"Your hostage theory! Then Doll Face just killed a *Boche!* If we were hostages, she'd be tried for murder. What about that?"

"But if not, what's the point of this insane counting? And why not liquidate us right now, what's stopping them?"

In fact not long ago, the day before yesterday, Doll Face had a fit in the *Appelplatz*: One person out of several thousand was missing. Today she aimed without blinking! Which shows that it's easier for a camel to pass through the eye of a needle than for one of us to understand how the Germans think . . .

They're sounding roll call. What is it now? I've been writing for quite a while. Sophie has gone to sleep. She's breathing heavily. In her sleep, her intellect leaves her. She's just a poor kid, exhausted and dirty. She's holding her arm folded over her bald head as if to protect it. I have to wake her up. Suddenly I'm worn out, overwhelmed, as if this weren't just my pal but all of humankind lying before me with cracked lips, hopeless, defenseless . . .

—

Geography lesson with my brother. He knows it's my weak subject. "Tell me where to find . . ." he begins, and then pauses for effect. He says a name. Is it a city, a country, an island? In my dream it seems that I've heard it before. My poor brain runs to extremes, my overtaxed memory wanders desperately between the Russian steppes, Greenland, and the Canary Islands, in a universe that's horribly vast and mysteriously divided. It's impossible for me (even when I'm awake) to remember anything clearly except the Italian boot and Africa, which looks like a boxing glove.

I pretend to think; he gives me an amused look and bends over the map again. I watch him incredulously. In this haughty, quiet boy I no longer recognize my little brother, three years younger than me; it's his face, but not his expression. Maybe he's changed, aged? Maybe it's Professor Wunch, grown young again? No, this is not my brother.

I'm awakened by doubt and distress, which I carry with me all day. And to top it off, Magda, the insolent *Stubendienst,* lashes me with a riding crop. I blubber. I can't get used to the idea that this bitch, that any bitch, should be able to touch me.

—

"The Russians are coming!"

"How do you know?"

"There wasn't any bread today."

"?"

"They're cornered, you see. So we're the ones who catch it."

"Oh, I see!"

I don't show any enthusiasm, and she gives me an annoyed look.

"If they stay cornered another three days," I say to her, "the Russians won't have anyone left to liberate."

"Matter of hours," she replies calmly. "They're very close. Don't you hear the cannons?"

"Yes, vaguely . . ."

Vertigo. In the afternoon everyone seems to have it. Could that be more cannons? Are we hearing things? Nothing stimulates the imagination like hunger.

Squatting in the sun in front of the barracks, utterly spent, we wait for the Russians.

—

The *Zählappel* continues late into the night. At dawn they drag us from our bunks. They count, they re-count. The Germans and their dogs take turns howling. Panic-stricken and bathed in sweat, the Slovaks fuss about between the ranks; they don't even remember to hit. We alone stand impassively in the general confusion, as if none of it concerned us.

It reminds me of a stack of bricks that we saw from the railroad car, in a station: rows carefully aligned; and all around, excited people yelling in a strange dialect.

Something's getting ready to happen. Everything's quiet, even the rumors. Nothing depends on us now. It's comforting, in a way. Perfect silence, like bricks.

—

They're evacuating us from Auschwitz. To where? Nobody knows. It might happen tomorrow, or this afternoon, or an hour from now. I'd be calm if I weren't worried about the fate of my journal. Our shoes will be given back to us after the disinfection. That's certain, apparently, but there's no way to stuff all this paper into them. Sophie suggests that I reread it carefully, ten times in a row, and write down one or two sentences per chapter as a memory aid. That would take just a few sheets. The idea isn't bad, but what about the time?

—

I'm four days away from Auschwitz, and for the first time I'm writing . . . in a *notebook*. Brown cover, two hundred pages. According to Sophie, there's no such thing as "providence," but it doesn't matter what name you stick on the luck that comes your way. There aren't any posters here, and the camouflage paper is black. It would have been the end of my notes, without a miracle.

Although, again according to Sophie, there wouldn't have been any miracle if I hadn't spotted the *Lagerkapo* with the notebook under his arm, if I didn't speak German, if I hadn't been harebrained enough to approach him.

He's almost bald, with a hooked nose. He stops and listens to my rambling story about a notebook that I'm expecting. I don't know what else I say, but I'm raving, to judge by the way he frowns at me; he's a well-bred person, since there's no slap. He continues on his way.

"Aber Herr Lagerkapo?"[1]

He stops. "What do you mean, you've been expecting this notebook? They just brought it to me."

He's irritated, but that doesn't diminish my surprise. He speaks German without either a Polish or a regional accent, and that must be what immediately reassures me; I've never heard speech like his, here where people only yap, and almost always in a rural dialect, even the officers. You wonder sometimes whether they're talking to their buddy or their dog.

How the heck do they understand one another in a Reich where there are more dialects than people?

It's also the first time that I've stood in front of an armband by choice.

"I have to write," I tell him. "I need a notebook. I'm a writer."

He looks at me with his eyes of faded blue. It's only too obvious that he wants to laugh, and so do I: Once I cool down, I can't help seeing myself as he sees me—as I see the others—in the dress that flaps around my skinny body, the two match sticks protruding from it, my bald head . . . irresistible!

"I'm a writer."

[1] But Mister Lagerkapo?

I burst out laughing, although he doesn't even smile.

He gives me the notebook. But instead of taking off, I search desperately for a phrase to explain my incongruous behavior. He absolves me with a friendly wink: "Okay, I understand."

I don't have anything to write with; I must still be a little punchy, because I can't remember how to say pencil in German. I explain with gestures. He rummages in his pockets and manages to extract a pencil.

And then he lets out a real laugh, which makes him look younger despite the deep wrinkles that crease his long, worn, ashen face (he's not an old geezer, though).

No Sophie on the bunk. I probably look overwrought, insane. No one says anything. They just move away, glancing sidelong at the notebook, cautious . . . as if it were a land mine.

If I had to make a profession of faith at this moment, I'd say: I believe in silence. I try to get up before everyone else. Not to write, but to savor these few hours of solitude that I steal from sleep.

But even during the day we're a long way from Auschwitz. Each of us has her own blanket, straw mattress, and pan; we're still in quarantine, on "holiday." Thanks to the notebook, I no longer have any excuse to be idle. It's high time I made my report—starting with when they drove us out of the barracks at Auschwitz and sent us, after interminable roll calls, across the dark camp between double rows of barbed wire, flanked by police dogs and clanking boots, blue with cold and shriveled like a procession of resuscitated mummies.

In the *Waschraum*, I found myself facing a razor that did not inspire confidence—the hand of the Polish woman wielding the instrument trembled alarmingly. In fact she nicked me in a particularly sensitive spot. I let out a yell, alone among the thousand and some being nicked. She looked at me in a puzzled way, the way she would look at a cat that started talking. But she paid more attention to her work. Irony of fate: She's hairy as a monkey, she who spends her life shaving others!

Our train was late. The arrival of a Belgian or Dutch convoy livened things up a little.

An indescribable meeting: "civilian" hair, "civilian" clothes, "civilian" horror at the sight of our bald, naked herd.

"Was ist das, ein Spital?"[1] I can still hear our group asking the same questions, staring with the same wide eyes.

[1] What is this, an asylum?

The same naked crowd had pressed around us three weeks earlier, when we got off at the Auschwitz station. They stared in the same incredulous and hungry way at our hair, our clothes, our suitcases . . .

On one side are the incredulous newcomers with their suitcases, and on the other is the naked, shaven crowd, looking more like a herd of cows than women. The meeting must always be the same. Except that this time we're the herd, and the fact that we joke instead of moo seems to surprise the long-haired ones. With their touching civilian logic they ask questions like tourists: "Are they madwomen?"

The Germans double over with laughter, the Poles sneer, and we ourselves giggle. It all happens for them like it did for us (imagination has its limits). After a few minutes they begin to reappear one after another, as naked and bald as we are, completely dumbfounded with dizziness and panic.

I remember the moment when, coming from the Waschraum, I noticed for the first time the crowd of bare skulls with their repulsive whiteness: You would have said a field of cabbages.

A hallucinatory spectacle; I must have spent a while out of touch, not making the connection between myself and that sea of shining skulls. "They're madwomen," I said to myself, and I waited. But the open door disgorged more heads of cabbage. Amazing! This illness always produces the same symptoms: the same protruding ears, the same waxy face, the same idiotic and twisted grin.

One of them pointed her finger at me: "My God, look at you!" All the while a blue vein stood out on her naked skull. That voice, I had heard it before; the monster reminded me of someone . . . Illus from *Miskolc!* Beautiful, blond Illus. (The sentry even offered to help her escape from the brickyard.)

I brought my hand up to my head, and suddenly everything became clear. She made a soothing gesture, as if to ease the awful moment that she herself had just gone through—she who had been shorn of the most magnificent head of hair—and tried with a touching eagerness to console me, who had lost only two pitiful braids.

"Who cares about hair," she said, "when we've lost everything, even the tears to cry. It grows back, you'll see, it grows back in a hurry."

I looked at her, speechless. If she could have seen herself! Those huge ears! And what an impossible shape to her skull!

It seemed to me that all the tortures, all the losses had been mild compared to this one! As if the barber had cut me off from myself.

Perhaps we make up a new species never before recorded in history; a typically Boche discovery, somewhere between a human being and a thing. The only human attribute that it retains is the ability to suffer; it is, more precisely: a *suffering thing*.

If anything happened to us, my notebook and me, this expression would be lost and that would be a shame. It might have been useful to a historian—unless our story remains without witnesses, like a hole in time, or so incredible that any testimony would be pointless.

But back to the Waschraum.

In three weeks, this is the second time they've shaved us. What falls from our heads is hardly more than half an inch long. Sorrow has given way to indifference; I remember above all an overwhelming desire to sit down, anywhere, so long as the place was dry and at a bearable temperature, because the cement was freezing.

We wait for the distribution of clothes, huddled together, almost glued to one another, trying to protect ourselves from the cold.

The Dutch shiver, not daring to get close together—novices ashamed of their nakedness. They don't dare look at us, although we stare at them shamelessly, in a good-natured way. A mocking voice calls out to them:

"So, my friends? Nudism isn't in style where you come from? We never get undressed anymore unless there are a few men around." She lets out a big laugh, so heartily that the several thousand "nudists" around her can't help doing the same, although there's no reason to rejoice. As evening falls, we feel more and more naked. This is how we'll spend the night. No sign of a train.

Clumped together like a single body, like a sort of monster that snores, whimpers, and coughs from a thousand throats. The Germans disperse us from time to time with blows of their riding crops. But we get right back together, because we fear the whips less than the cold.

The daytime is more bearable because it's the month of June, and because of this unique and comical creature who "never gets undressed anymore unless there are a few men around . . ."

And now suddenly I want to put everything aside and concentrate on her.

Imagine the body of a boy, tall, thin, and flat-chested, on pillars that could support a cathedral and its towers. Despite this massive base—out of indifference, or perhaps alarmed by her own height—she curves her back, which makes her stomach stick out and gives her silhouette the shape of an S. It may be simply her basic impudence expressing itself in her nonchalant posture, as it does in her mimicry and in her every utterance; without that sort of outlandish humor she might be just a rather ordinary, tall, bald girl. Yet I tend to think that she was born an exuberant person; as if the world wasn't big enough for her and she felt the need to constantly break out . . .

She answers to the pleasant name of Juliette.

From up close she seems really young, but what does that matter? Prodigies are beyond time. Am I exaggerating? Possibly. But isn't she herself a sort of exaggeration, the product of an uncontrolled imagination?

Nevertheless, the woman who gave birth to her doesn't seem to be overly burdened with imagination. A person whose exceptional age, baldness, motherliness, and talkativeness make her hard to describe. She, too, seems an exaggeration, on the verge of senility! She protests and complains constantly, about the cold, the barber, the "unspeakable" treatment that the Nazis have inflicted on her and her daughter, the "disgusting" cement. At home, at her house in S.— where we're all invited, by the way—the floor shines like a mirror. German culture! What a disappointment to her, who spent her vacation every year at Baden-Baden and has read *Faust*! How could this nation, which is so concerned with hygiene, build such awful latrines! The war, deportation, it's all hard on her nerves! It interferes with the development of her daughter, who is exceptionally gifted for the stage; we should have seen her with her golden curls playing the fairy in the school performance of *Csongor and Tünde*! She herself, in her youth, was a hit in a benefit show. It was certainly from her that the child inherited her artistic abilities.

But the "child" absolutely denies having inherited anything from her at all. She's her father's daughter; he was a womanizer, a gambler, a liar. But what class!

"It must be sclerosis," she explains to us in front of her mother, who is petrified by the general hilarity. "It's true that once, way back when, she spent her vacation at Baden-Baden. As for *Faust,* all she knows is the title; apart from recipes, she only reads Agatha Christie. Golden curls, ha, ha, ha! That's a good one! An unspeakable mop like you rarely see."

She's almost glad to be rid of it. It's the only good thing the Germans have done for her.

In *Csongor and Tünde* she was indeed a hit, but of course in the role of the witch. Built the way she is, and with her cabbie's voice, ingenues are not really her thing. With a few movements of her hips, swinging her outlandish silhouette, she evokes the delicate good fairy so hilariously that the naked audience is beside itself with laughter.

But we hardly have time to pull ourselves together when in place of the delicate fairy there appears an awful shrew, hunchbacked and limping: Mirigy, the witch. There's an evil light in her squinting eyes, and her twisted mouth spews horrible insults (the more sensitive retreat). All at once she straightens up, pale, with burning eyes and an accusatory look, stares at a point in space, and breaks into a biting laugh. For a second the huge, packed room holds its breath.

"Am I a prisoner? No . . . But then what is this lackey doing outside my door? Here he is!"[1]

With a sweeping gesture she opens an imaginary door, grabs me—I'm within reach—and pushes me to the front.

For a moment I stand disconcerted before my royal prisoner, suffering the contempt aimed at me from every direction. I'm dismissed with a majestic wave of the hand, and the unfortunate son of the great emperor gives a triumphant laugh at having unmasked (thanks to me, the spy) that old scoundrel Metternich.

"O naive prince of Reichstadt!"

That's the only line that she's kept from Rostand's play. But who cares about the words! I've seen the play several times, even at the national theater in Budapest with Hilda Gobbi. She was magnificent in her princely trappings—and she was a huge hit—but I don't think I've ever seen a real audience in a real

[1] The scene is from *L'Aiglon* (The Young Eagle), a play about Napoleon II. The young hero is traditionally played by a woman.

theater charmed like we were, naked on the naked stone, during that enchanting improvisation.

Another four or five pages on the "prodigy." Then I changed my mind and tore them out. It seemed to me that this scatterbrain took up too much room in my thoughts and in my notes, that after all we were right in the middle of a disaster the like of which hasn't been seen since the Flood—in short that she was making me neglect the disaster in some way (or else I have trouble accepting other people's success wherever it happens, even in the middle of a disaster).

In our new camp we're in quarantine. At least it allows me to finish my "travel report." I have to hurry; new material is accumulating dangerously, and I'm barely able to keep up with the daily events that besiege me: the Zählappel, my bunk mates, the fact that I tripped over a skull this morning. This camp is located on the site of a former Jewish cemetery; sometimes you come across a rib, sometimes a tibia. One day I stumbled over a complete set of dentures.

You get used to it, like the dust and the mud; you walk on it or shove it away with your foot. The poor soul whose bones crack under our feet will forgive us, I hope; in our place, would he act differently? I'd almost be afraid we might lose our ability to be astonished, if the person who spent her summers at Baden-Baden and gave birth to a prodigy wasn't there to be astonished for us.

She squats all day long on the steps of the barracks and shows everyone who passes a fragment of skull that she found in the sand. She sighs.

"What do you think of this?" She loses herself in reflections à la Hamlet. "Behold what is man and what can become of him!"

If there aren't too many people, she bends close to your ear and whispers in a shaken voice:

"Tell me, do you think they're really going to kill us?"

"Come on, now, what an idea!"

"And the Polish and German and Slovakian Jews?"

"That's different."

"Why is it different?"

"Because!"

I make myself scarce, in the conviction that this old bat will get herself killed one of these days. The only way she could avoid that disastrous fate would be to become mute.

Which reminds me of an episode at Auschwitz that I haven't written about (you can't write about everything).

Scene: the Waschraum.

Heroine: Juliette.

She's in the process of improvising an operatic scene, a very amusing soprano-tenor duet; she performs the contortions of the lips with almost no sound; she raises her eyes to the ceiling and gargles a while,

for an audience that's as worn out from laughter as
from hunger. Then suddenly in the middle of a fio-
ritura she stops, which only increases the mirth.

"What's happening?" she asks in her raucous voice.

Thinking it's a new number, the crowd continues
to laugh. But soon we hear something that's certainly
not part of the show: somewhere fairly near by, regular thuds as if someone were banging on the wall.
Now that I'm paying attention, it seems to me that
I've been aware of them before, these Auschwitz
noises, and the uneasiness that they cause. I'm not
talking about the racket that we live with constantly—
that we make—but the indistinct sounds that reach us
by fits and starts, whose source we don't know, that
we sometimes think we've imagined, as if somewhere
not very far from us a parallel life were going on.
(What if it's only the muffled echo of our agonies?)

Silence: That just means the difference between
two sorts of racket, one close and familiar, the other
invisible and disturbing.

For the first few weeks I hardly closed my eyes.
The fear of being awakened by mysterious cries and
blows kept me on the alert all night. I spied, I
peeked, I listened to everything, and yet in the morning it seemed to me that I had been dreaming. Finally
I would succumb to fatigue and the real dreams would
come; everything would get jumbled together, and I

couldn't say which was harder for me to take: what I heard awake or in dreams.

What's the matter with her?

"Something's about to happen here," she screams. "Otherwise, why have they kept us naked for two days?"

She leans on the handle of the door that has never been locked, and it doesn't move. She hits it and shakes it.

"Stop!" someone shouts.

Then we all start yelling. It's the best we can do against the fear. "Ideas" are contagious, and this nut case would be smart to keep hers to herself if she doesn't want to be lynched. But she isn't ready to calm down. Her fists continue to hammer on the iron door, while people shove her, pull her, hit her, and her poor mother clings to her and sobs.

The change from opera parody to hysterics happened almost without transition. How did that laughing group transform in no time at all into a vicious mob? And how did it calm down just as suddenly? I was there and yet I can't explain how, in the space of a few seconds, so many distinct individuals can become such a horribly single *thing*.

The night passed without any other incidents. I don't believe many were able to sleep. One single time I heard peaceful and regular snoring; it was Juliette. Her old mother, propped on her elbow nearby, watched over her.

It was still dark when the lock creaked. For a moment I remained motionless, with my eyes closed, wrapped in the night. I tried to imagine that I had been dead for a long time and that all this was only the "afterlife"—where nothing could touch me anymore. I hardly breathed at all. The impassiveness of nonbeing was coming over me, when suddenly a very earthly voice, Sophie's, reached me.

"Get up, they're handing out clothes!"

I took off like a bullet.

—

Shivering but with a light heart, I lean against the wall of the railroad car in my new dress, where five like me could fit comfortably. Where are they taking us? It doesn't matter! Since it's in order to *exist* somewhere . . . My heart beats with the rhythm of the wheels: "I'm alive, I'm alive."

—

But you get accustomed to *existing*. Then come the cold, the hunger, and these dirty, nasty boards! After half an hour we look like black cats. No way to get warm. In the huge cattle car there are only twenty of us, and if we huddle against one another, someone remains at the end of the line with her back exposed to the night, and that someone is usually me, the littlest and skinniest. They always push me back.

"Stop fidgeting, you're not a child anymore."

Is that any reason to catch my death?

I don't know how many days and nights we traveled. Three . . . five? As for food, we got some twice. We only saw daylight when we emptied the excrement bucket. At the end we no longer had the strength to talk; we no longer even tried to get warm. I didn't even have the strength to imagine that I'd been dead for a long time. When the door of the car finally opened, we crashed onto the platform, stiff as boards.

Poland, bleak and soaking wet. The rain hits our shaven heads in big drops and gently spreads out.

While the column is forming, I see pigs coming out of one of the cars. They amble down the ladder set up for them: well cared for, clean, pink. Where did all these fat pigs come from, in such a thin country?

Finally we set out, each group of twenty flanked by a guard who's tired and gloomy, like the weather.

One of them reveals that the camp is two and a half miles away; we're going to Plaszow, on the outskirts of Cracow.

What they call "Cracow" is so heartrending that as we go through it I try to keep my eyes closed; despite the intact houses that emerge from the ruins, it's hard to believe that this desert of stones, with huge mud-filled craters blocking our way, was once a city. Sometimes a face appears at a window; astonished at the sight of this bald herd, it withdraws discreetly when it senses that it's being observed. I envy those faces; the rain doesn't touch them. They may be alone in a room, watching us with compassion from the window. They still have things to lose.

Uniforms everywhere. They swarm over the rubble, they shout, they laugh unpleasantly. They go so well with the scenery! Cities destroyed, lives destroyed—their work on an earth that is wounded by their footsteps, fouled by their breath.

We walk in the nonexistent streets of a city that is no more. The rain itself seems to shiver on our bodies. I close my eyes, hold on to my neighbors, and concentrate on the images in colored circles that play under my eyelids or somewhere in the air in front of me. And as incredible as it may seem, the images are all colorful and sunlit: A bright green lawn, and around a fountain a circle of people, escaped from the middle of the forest, turning in tighter and tighter spirals. Is it vertigo again? A magnificent door made of white beech. A stone bench carved with animals and flowers. I open my eyes.

The door in front of me is made of iron. It isn't

carved; a poster bears the familiar inscription on a red background: "Arbeit Macht Frei."[1] The guard makes his report and a whole crowd of black rain slickers runs up to greet us. They count and recount us excitedly, as if we were pennies.

We walk along an avenue between two rows of electric poles. They're lined up ahead of us, straight, as if standing at attention.

The road is covered with small white gravel. As we advance I suddenly notice a hill, very nearby, a stone's throw away.

"The hill," I say.

I hold out my hand as if to show this surprise to my rank of five. But the zombies dragging along beside me don't even raise their heads.

"Look at the hill!"

I nudge one of them, who's sleeping as she walks.

"So what?" she mutters.

Her voice is sepulchral, her eyes hollow; I let it drop.

All of a sudden I understand what the feeling of absence is that I carry around with me so unhappily: the absence of green.

At Auschwitz I didn't see any trees, and none on this long Polish road, either; not one, from the time they first put me on a train. Strange that I hadn't no-

[1] Work Will Make You Free.

ticed it. Are they even "exterminating" the trees? Shit. As we approach the hill, the distance from Auschwitz increases and so does hope; my hill is only a knoll, a poor, bare mound . . .

Like everywhere, the barracks are surrounded by a fenced-in area. But I have to admit that they seem less frightening than those at Auschwitz! Everything looks temporary and makeshift. The buildings look like huts, and the prisoners in their black slickers, wearing polished black boots, can hardly be distinguished from their keepers.

The Polish women are beautiful, the men well built. Despite the bad weather and our great fatigue, we eye them with a nostalgic curiosity. We're disconcerted by their "elegance."

Our arrival causes a veritable onslaught. We find ourselves surrounded, crowded by all these "slickers." They gesticulate, they laugh, they speak to us in their melodious language. We can only answer with laughter.

At a long table five women with five sheets of paper take down our information by groups of five. Having done so, they hand us registration slips with red numbers. Mine is 1555. We once again have names, dates of birth, professions. I see myself with a new respect. To be registered, to count somewhere—the feeling of being legal!

Perhaps it has spent its last drops; its work done, the rain stops. To finish the job it sends us a blast of wind. A current of frigid air blows across the square, which is open on all sides, puffing out our clothes and making them snap like wet flags.

I feel my throat swelling, and shivers that are freezing one minute and burning the next. Sophie firmly prophesies: pneumonia! Just at the moment when our prospects were improving: a life as respectable, *lawful* prisoners . . .

Nature, fortunately, is less logical than Sophie. Out of the two thousand people who arrived after a trip of several days in a railroad car and a two-and-a-half-mile walk in a torrential rain, followed by several hours spent standing in wet clothes, there were only two mild cases of flu.

Sophie and I are in top form.

If I say, "We rested," I'm still a long way from conveying the reality. Can you put into words the joyful creaking of stiff bones, the hymn of praise from constricted lungs and cramped backs, the ecstatic shivers of an entire aching body abandoned to the sweet embrace of a straw mattress and a warm blanket?

We underwent a real metamorphosis: We turned into marmots. From dawn till midnight and from midnight till dawn we did nothing but snore in unison.

Anyone who has not yet attended the evening Zählappel knows nothing about Plaszow. We newcomers are still in quarantine, and we watch this ostentatious show from our windows. The lighted barracks look like real houses, and the deportees, dressed like sportsmen, look like real women and real men who might have gathered for a real reason in the square of a real town. In the middle of the square stands a post, at the top of which flies a black flag with a swastika; but not always. Its disappearance from the post is the signal for a mournful ceremony.

Hanging is part of the local color. It's a tradition at Plaszow, a "method" that the camp commandant favors. It's at his express request that the "politicals" from Cracow and other Polish prisons are sent to Plaszow; among them are women, high-school students, sometimes even children. Usually it's an imprudent word, a look, or just the suspicion that they don't love the Reich, that has brought them to the post.

A revolver could do the job just as well, but the commandant of Plaszow loves pageantry; he's an aesthete.

That's why these poor devils have the "honor" of choking to death in a solemn setting before thousands of spectators.

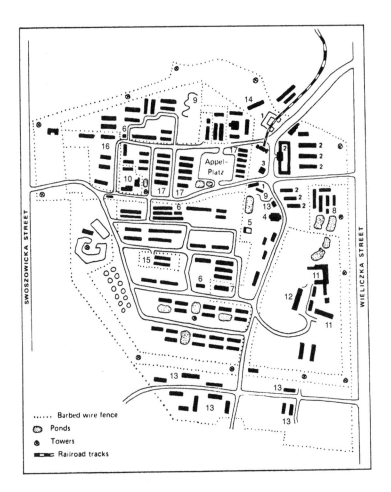

Cracow-Plaszow Concentration Camp

1 Offices	7 Brick warehouse	13 Germans' house
2 Soldiers' quarters	8 Balb warehouse	14 Hospital for SS
3 Gray house	9 Stone quarry	15 Building area
4 Goeth's villa	10 Kitchen	16 Camp hospital
5 Dogs' house	11 Stables	17 Barracks
6 Latrine	12 Garage	

They say that the commandant's aestheticism goes so far that one day he blew a girl's brains out because her laces weren't properly tied. According to the natives, he's a gambler, temperamental, one of those refined sadists who treats himself to Mozart and Bach after each hanging. At the moment he seems to be staying away from the camp. Could he be feeling out of sorts? Or is it because of the Allies' untimely advance? We mustn't rejoice too soon; we'll still be treated to some alarming spectacles.

We're all at the window watching this sort of folk festival: the women in white scarves and the men in black, shiny boots. The scarves in front and the boots behind—they form two perfectly aligned squares around the post. White and black, the color of tombstones, and the post with the flag floating in the wind reminds you of a gaunt monk performing a strange ceremony of the living dead.

—

I've forgotten to talk about the *Kapos*. There's a man with an armband at the front of each line, and three or four others who move about freely in the middle of the square. They walk around, looking tired and playing with their whips, while the Kapos of lower rank struggle to count. They have the highest status among the detainees, except for the *Lagerälteste*.

The Lagerälteste!

Imagine a chicken half plucked, half platinum blond; when she turns around you see the terrifying face of an old monkey-woman, sad and garishly made up. She breaks into solitary laughter in a way that makes our blood run cold. Is it to give herself courage? Or to show off her impeccable teeth?

This female Janus, half monkey and half chicken, who must have failed to reach normal size because of a childhood illness, is still able to take a German's arm, thanks to very high heels that bring her up to the elbow of an average *Fritz;* she's only half Jewish according to some, a fourth according to others. They claim that she has the commandant in her pocket, that her exuberant laughter is matched by an inventive and insatiable viciousness. In truth, how could you be sweet and upright with a mug like hers? The dwarf and the camp. Aren't they destined to do well together—like two tumors of the same disease?

—

Today during roll call I recognized, among the few men with armbands who are allowed to move around, my friend with the notebook. (How could I have guessed that I was throwing myself at a divinity of the highest rank?) I very much wanted to make a sign to him, if only to see whether he recognized me.

I know what the price is for any spot on that "Olympus." But even so, nobody forced him to give me the notebook! ("Or become a Lagerkapo," Sophie observes). Am I too tolerant, the height of opportunism? Certainty frightens me—my own arguments frighten me when I'm alone with them. As if solitude threw everything into question. If I held in my hands my "soul," my "conscience," the very essence of my humanity, would I find anything consistent and solid in it? Except for things like this: I firmly detest the Fritzes; I would detest them even if I were German and free, even if they didn't present the least threat to me or mine. They offend everything in me that makes me different from a sheep.

—

You can hear the cannons. They're coming, they're coming, they're coming! What else could it mean? If I could believe just one hundredth of the news that reaches the barracks every day as the "latest" and the "most certain."

—

By all indications, they should have arrived yesterday at noon. And still nothing! The Boche don't seem overly worried. Could they have stopped? Just outside Cracow? If only they knew that we literally wither away when the noise of the cannons stops! At the first shot everything revives.

I'm chattering; just a way of trying to quiet my worry; in vain. It's said that they're going to transport us away from the front, to somewhere in the mother country.

That's what we needed: the mother country!

No news of any importance. I relate the most insignificant items simply to keep myself busy, starting with the pan. Sophie found a saucepan; she swore that it wasn't used for garbage, although I hadn't asked. Doubts about its origin didn't stop me from enthusiastically helping restore it from the status of scrap metal to that of a utensil. And I can say, not without a certain pride: The pan is usable. And since we devoted a portion of our bread ration for the noble purpose of plugging holes, it's flawless. It's true that so far we've only used it to drink water, and we're a little concerned about its "resistance" to hot liquid.

They're "calling." I'll continue after "lunch."

The pan is watertight; the soup stays at the same level. It's been a while since we filled it, but we haven't touched it.

Oh, the "menus" at Auschwitz! We suspected sand in the bread sometimes, but never pebbles like here; they gurgle in this dishwater like potatoes in a stew.

There are some that slide imperceptibly into the stomach and behave themselves so well there that you don't even notice them. But most of them slyly let themselves be swallowed and begin to make themselves known later, in your throat or in your stomach. With me it's in my back, I have no idea why. Knowing that it would be useless to call for help, I wait for the end, sweating.

Sophie, the marmot, didn't close her eyes all night; a piece of gravel as big as a fingernail supposedly slipped into her stomach.

"How do you know it's the size of a fingernail?"

"It showed up for a second in my spoon, then I didn't see it anymore."

Evidently. She was transparent, to the point that her freckles had turned yellow; her eyes were burning; her breathing was ragged.

I held her hand for half the night. "What's the point? You get some rest at least," she suggested selflessly. But her voice was so doleful that I protested strongly: "What does one night matter?" I don't know how long I lasted. When I woke up, there wasn't a trace of Sophie, and I was crushed when I saw her empty place. Poor Sophie, so dear, so faithful! How many times I've betrayed you in my thoughts and even in my journal. No, from now on everything will be different! If only I see you alive again! I found her slumped over a basin; she was trying to vomit.

"Look, the pebble!" I cried, suddenly "enlightened" as I bent over the basin.

She looked at me in dismay and bent over the opening. After a while she straightened up, excited.

"Yes, I saw it!"

"Don't you feel better?"

I almost fell into the basin pretending to examine the hole, to hide my face, which was twisted with laughter.

"Yes," she said, "I'm a whole new woman."

And indeed she revived before my eyes: Her voice became firm, her freckles darkened again.

I didn't see the pebble. I'm tempted to admit my bluff, but I refrain for fear that she'll start to feel it weighing on her stomach again.

My phobia about pebbles is appeased. This dishwater is undrinkable in any case. Even rest becomes exhausting in the long run, and leaves too much time for hunger.

Oh, to sink my teeth into some substantial food . . . meat, a loaf of bread, cheese! This obsession is driving me crazy. I think about my friend with the notebook, the man with the sad, kind look, who may at this moment be devouring roast beef with fried potatoes.

The idea occurs to me that beggars aren't aware of their humiliation, or don't care about it. It exists only in the minds of the well fed. Hunger overwhelms everything.

———

Poor, poor Félicie. Félicie is in charge of our barracks; she slapped me today. That's obviously not a reason to feel sorry for her. You don't feel sorry for Félicie for one reason or another, she's just pitiful, period. When I saw her for the first time she immediately reminded me of a classmate, the most unfortunate creature who ever sat on the benches of the Jewish high school.

Not that she was sick, or a poor orphan—she didn't lack for anything, but an unseen doom hovered over her head and made sure her pencil box was the one that fell with a crash during Latin composition. She was the one whose garter belt came unhooked just at the moment when she was called up to the blackboard; although she was always hurrying, she never failed to arrive late; and so on.

It was those little things that made her behavior hesitant or hasty and gave her a furtive and tormented expression, as if she was always preparing to defend herself from an unexpected attack. That's the expression that Félicie, the head of our barracks, wears; she dreads so many things at the same time! But it has never occurred to her that there might be any difference between a shaven head and her straw mattress. To her we're transparent, but she doesn't know that transparency is a great strength here, and that higher than the Fritzes, the dwarf, and the Kapos, there is a secret commando unit: an army of letters that I command in silence. The important heads that I lop off every day, with no problem! The ordinary creeps before whom I hesitate—like Félicie (the last one to suspect that her slap is about to make it into history).

When she slapped me she didn't even look at me. It's true that I wasn't the one who hollered. But who could tell, in the confusion, and I was within reach.

This morning she was more worked up than usual, which was understandable since the roll call hadn't come out right. The German slapped her twice, in front of us: German slaps, entirely different from the flicks of her own withered hands!

Poor jerk! She's always threatening us with astounding things: If we don't get out of bed right away, she'll have us sent forthwith to Dachau to the gas chamber, she'll have us locked up, shot, etc. And all this in a little thin voice ready to break. I haven't the slightest idea how she made herself a "place in the sun"; it gets her quite a bit of extra bread and jam, but little "glory." Nevertheless she clings to it fiercely. Hence her incoherent, tense, excessive manner. She arrives two hours before roll call, counts and recounts us twenty-five times, and still she's the only *Block-älteste* who inevitably gets fouled up. The Germans have made her the butt of their jokes, and she rarely gets through it without a smack. She takes it out on us. This morning, after the slap in question, I grabbed her arm. I don't know how it happened, but suddenly I felt beneath my fingers something like the fragile bone of a struggling bird. I let go right away. She made a gesture as if she wanted to hit me again, then she must have changed her mind and she turned on her heel and left; maybe she didn't think she could maintain her dignity in the face of a confrontation . . .

Note: This was the first slap at the camp that didn't bother me. Because it came from Félicie, and because I defended myself? I'm beginning to know the tune, to *get used to it*. The "meaningless conceits" are falling one after another . . . My "I," excitable and vindictive, is ready to withdraw from all those matters that don't concern it, and there's only one matter that concerns me here: my notebook. *Here*, nobody hurts me or touches me, only my skin; and every day I'm closer to being nothing but skin!

—

I read Sophie a few passages from my notes. She thought they weren't bad, but that my old journals were more "personal."

I haven't talked about them yet; I've been keeping these notes since the age of eleven. I left six big notebooks with the concierge, in a book bag, before I started at the Jewish high school in Miskolc. I hope she's taking care of them! I have nightmares about it that recur with variations: I'm walking somewhere in a square (near the municipal theater in N.). I'm hugging my notebooks tightly, it's windy and I'm going along carefully; yet I know for a fact that *it* will happen, that it's inevitable. And when the notebooks start to slide, I don't make any effort to hold on to them. I watch the pages being scattered by the wind, marked by the footprints of passersby. It's as if I were at my own funeral and didn't have the strength to shout, "Hey, I'm alive!"

Anyone who has never felt the irresistible need to write down everything he thinks, sees, and touches will perhaps accuse me of exaggerating, but it's true. I've had long periods when I only existed *through* and *for* my journal. I often scribbled under the desk in class, or in the bathroom, because my journal was "outlawed" on the grounds that it interfered with my

appetite and my sleep, to say nothing of my home-
work. Everything that happened to me only happened through being written down. My real life was
only a sort of servant, the supplier of my "written"
life.

But life went too fast, events always got ahead of
me; I ran desperately after them, and the unequal
struggle exhausted me.

Often, in the middle of a conversation, I wanted to
get up and rush to my journal, or interrupt the person
I was talking to and ask him to repeat what he'd just
said ten minutes before. I couldn't relax until I had
properly set things down in my notebook; my blackest
despairs turned into fond memories if I devoted a few
well-written pages to them. Which reminds me of an
affair of the heart that I experienced just a few
months ago.

The object of my passion, the brother of one of my
friends, a tall, taciturn boy, fascinated me. He was said
to be a painter. He had a prominent chin, and when
he laughed his lower teeth hid the upper row; I was
enchanted by that particular shape of his face, as if it
were a work of art in itself.

I thought I was being scorned, but in fact he hadn't
even noticed me.

That's how my first and only love letter came to be.
I worked on it for a day and a night, and as I did so I
constantly grew in my own eyes; I found myself

splendid, subtle, and so radiant that the object of my passion lost all interest. The idea of sending the letter never occurred to me.

I know that my notebook isn't well thought of on the bunk, that it could be discovered and destroyed at any moment—and that I would go on vegetating, waiting for the soup, with the disturbing knowledge that I'd have to do it all over, rescue it all from chaos, create myself again from A to Z.

The important thing: two observations by Sophie.

1. It's obvious that I'm not writing for myself.

2. Yet I dwell on myself, on details that concern only me. The style is careless, in places.

I admit it, I'm an incomplete witness, but otherwise how could I get through this experience without losing my mind? I observe in particular this crumb of the camp that is me, and the crumbs around me. No, how could I hope to give a complete view of the camp? (Like emptying the ocean with a ladle.)

My style leaves something to be desired. It's not because of carelessness. No. There are pages that I've recopied four times. Every line reeks of sweat, inevitably!

Often I don't manage to assemble my thoughts except by desperately hard work, for lack of inspiration! Writing when you're famished is not the same as in the bathtub.

I sound like I'm bragging! The truth is that it's a

constant struggle between my fatigue and the horrible "you must." Sometimes the latter gains the upper hand. I don't like to write. But I must!

Let me therefore briefly answer the question to which I may return another time: I'm not writing for myself, that goes without saying. I hope that these notes will be part of the evidence, on the day of reckoning! But even if I knew that I was to be my only reader, I would still write! I would take the same trouble to find the right word, the strongest word.

—

I've lost track of the man with the notebook.

We're still in quarantine, or rather in quarantine among the quarantined. The old barbed wire has been surrounded by new; are they really afraid we'll contaminate the natives? (How?)

Which doesn't stop us from gossiping the whole blessed day across the double barbed wire. Stories that make the hair stand up on our bald heads!

The poor natives! For them we're "virgin territory," the dreamed-of opportunity to soothe their ailing memories. They can't stop talking! One would say that at Plaszow the more relatives you've had who were hanged, buried alive, or shot, the more respectable you are. It's like listening to the Slovaks at Auschwitz. They all begin with the bread and butter

that we were devouring while their people . . .
They barely disguise their low opinion of the "glut-
tons" that we used to be. Perhaps they only come to
the barbed wire to throw it in our faces: the bread and
butter, and the fact that we let ourselves be rounded
up like sheep, that we didn't hide weapons, that we
didn't escape from the ghetto, and that not one of our
people ever liquidated a Fritz.

One of us lost her temper one day and retorted that
with or without "resistance" we were all in the same
fix!

They all started hollering at the same time. They
threatened us with their fists, they spat, they called us
"parasites, phooey!" We were stuffing ourselves with
foie gras while they, the fighters, were being massacred by the thousands, their children were being
thrown alive into the flames, etc.

Someone observing us from outside would probably
have been surprised to see the "fighters" dressed like
horsemen, their women carefully made up, and the
lucky "foie gras eaters" bald and emaciated.

That being said, it seems that the Warsaw ghetto
did in fact revolt. These horsemen and their made-up
ladies did shoot at the Fritzes, and only succumbed
because of superior numbers, while the idea of resistance didn't even occur to us.

"How many Boche have you liquidated?" Always

the same question, followed by the same arrogant grin.

We had no weapons, of course, except fingernails, teeth, and, at the brickyard, bricks by the thousands. There were twenty thousand of us, and a dozen guards . . . One day, in a small group, I even raised the question: "What if each of us picked up a brick?"

That set off a fuss something terrible! "We must isolate the irresponsible elements, they *irritate the authorities.*"

If we had all expected to be hanged in the next few minutes and somebody had shouted, "Forward! Spit, bite, claw! We have nothing to lose!" nobody would have budged, for fear that they would *irritate the authorities.* "Dignity" is only a word, perhaps, but "submission" is sickeningly real.

These insufferable Poles know something about that.

—

Around the barbed wire, a new invasion by the natives. Only one thing seems to be greater than their sufferings: the desire to talk about them. What drives us to the barbed wire, we the shorn ones, is also *desire.* But it's a different desire.

Despite their tragic past, they eat their fill every day; they might despise us even more if they realized that the news that there won't be any bread today (a miscalculation in the kitchen) upsets us more than the drama of an entire Polish family being massacred.

That's what the satiated will never be able to understand. The difference between a full belly and an empty belly is perhaps the greatest difference that there has ever been on earth. How else can you explain these well-fed martyrs' impassiveness when we look at them like greedy and shamefaced beggars? Sometimes they throw slices of snow-white bread. But it only leads to hostility and arguments. What's a tiny tidbit to our gluttonous appetites?

A while ago we noticed a larger than usual gathering. Sophie and I made our way through to the barbed wire. On the Polish side a man of about forty was eating fatback between two slices of white bread, which would have been enough to explain the mob—but there was something else.

As he nibbled distractedly at his bread, he told how he had lost his only son a few weeks before we arrived.

He was the darling of the entire camp. This was where he had grown up, the first and only Jewish child to be saved at Plaszow. When he was barely twelve years old he had watched the massacre of his mother and sister; he had been hidden in mattresses and under beds until he was seventeen years old and fit for work, when he was finally able to appear in broad daylight after long maneuvering, a real conspiracy. But the boy was alive, he was handsome and strong, and this man was the only father who had a son in the camp.

One day when he came back from work he couldn't find the boy. When he saw him again it was in the Appelplatz, between two Fritzes. The boy was a bloody heap, still struggling.

When the commandant appeared on his white horse (an exceptional thing for roll call), the father knew that all was lost, and had only one desire: for it to be over quickly.

But the colossus, who loved ceremony, discoursed for half an hour from atop his mount, about "Bolshevik agitation," about the "historic mission of the German race," etc. (all this in front of the "Juden-Hunde"!).[1]

The father didn't see the rest, because his companions closed in around him. But he heard his son gasping, then noise and agitation; the boy had managed to break the rope, had fallen to the ground and begged to be finished off with a bullet. His prayer was not answered. It all started again, and during the next several minutes he implored the God of Abraham to take away his reason—in vain.

[1] Jewish dogs.

The father finished his story with these words: "And I'm alive."

And eating, I thought.

He still held the fatback sandwich in his hand.

"In fact," remarked Sophie, "the sandwich that he kept nibbling impressed me more than his story."

—

No more news, except for one unpleasant item: For several days the Polish Christians (this is how we learned that among the polished boots and the white scarves there are also some of the "pure race") have not been allowed to go to work in the city, because their factory has been bombed.

Vitamin J (the Jewish vitamin, as we call news from the front) therefore no longer arrives. The natives wait, demoralized, prey to black forebodings. For some time now only the sparrows approach the barbed wire.

I no longer think about the man with the notebook. I come back to him only to make it clear: The Poles must be scratched out of the chapter entitled "Hope." They've never cared about us, and now they're not doing too well either. The goyim furnished them not only vitamin J, but also food, clothes, and zlotys. A Polish woman showed a bill to us, too.

The zloty passed from hand to hand; we were all as eager as Hottentots to touch it. The Polish woman laughed and gave us the zloty. It was a devalued bill, perhaps, or else she wanted to treat herself to the "show." Someone followed her around and explained that she, too, used to go shopping, had hair, and so on. The whole time she was weeping, as if she didn't expect to be believed, as if she didn't really believe it herself.

The barracks is unanimous in detesting the Poles. As for me, what frightens me is unanimity. I can't love or hate a group, and I'll never be able to, even with the Germans. I'm as powerless before a group as before a tiger.

—

I haven't yet had the pleasure of visiting the Plaszow market. They say that a terrible animation reigns there. Everyone is buying desperately; the watchword is to transform every zloty into food.

What luck not to have that sort of worries! In quarantine we practice a primitive commerce: two portions of soup for half a loaf of bread, a piece of soap equals half a soup, etc.

Since I know that on the other side of the barbed wire no one is stuffing himself, I manage to endure my empty stomach patiently.

—

The whole camp is waiting with bated breath, as in a fortress whose assault is imminent.

—

There's a lot more to tell, among other things: The quarantine has been lifted. We circulate freely in the camp. I haven't yet taken advantage of my "freedom," I don't have the time; I'm working as fast as I can, trying to finish my Auschwitz journal; tedious, but urgent. We don't know anything about the work that awaits us outside, except that we're not here to rest, nor to swallow soup and horrible stories.

The Christians have gone back to work, cleaning up the rubble of their factory. An idea nags at me relentlessly: to get my journal taken out by one of the goyim. Why shouldn't there be someone among them who would do it?

According to Sophie, of all my "ideas" that have ever frightened her, this is the most foolish.

We'll see.

—

A minor dispute with Ruchi Falk. I moan and cry out in my sleep; I'm sorry, but I'm not the mistress of my dreams. And it's not for her to give me a hard time about it!

That works out well; I was just thinking about describing my neighbors on the bunk.

So let's begin with the Falks.

Nature exaggerated greatly in their case; she must have been in a special mood to deck them out with trunks (annoying resemblance to the elephant, a rather likable beast). The prototype comes in three versions—at three different ages—with the same hard, furtive eyes, the same narrow forehead, the same voraciousness, the same enormous and sordid vitality. They'll make it out of the camp alive, there's no doubt, and if the planet should be destroyed by some cataclysm or other, I can see the three trunks now, the first things to emerge from the destruction, sniffing the air—or whatever replaces it—for possible "deals."

Each member of the "monstrous coalition" has her precise function. The boss is Ruchi, the oldest and strongest. Anytime there's a need to shove, elbow, or grab something instantly before someone else does, she's unrivaled.

Feigele's asset is sex appeal. She's the one whose duty it is to show her dimples (her even more ill-favored sisters place insane hope in them). You should see her acting the innocent, with her little weasel eyes, prattling to any Pole who'll listen that there were seven of them at home—nine, counting their parents—and that the three of them are the only ones left, so young, so defenseless.

Surele is the chameleon of the team. She changes her shape, her age, and her state of health at will. A weak and growing child if there's something left at the bottom of the soup pot, gravely ill if it's necessary to go out in bad weather, and she's fresh as a flower when a paid job presents itself (planting tomatoes around the Polish barracks or carrying the food bowls, for example).

Sometimes she's old and feeble. In that case they tie beneath her chin the black scarf that they cadged from a Polish woman (and which usually serves, in the form of a turban, to enhance Feigele's sex appeal). With the two weeping sisters supporting her solicitously, you have something that can extort a second helping of soup from the most hard-hearted cook!

Not surprising that this trio has, beginning at Auschwitz, risen to the post of Stubendienst. Félicie had barely appeared at the door of the barracks when she ran into the tribe in full battle array, standing before that indecisive creature like fate itself. She didn't try to resist; she seemed to recognize that these frightening people should distribute the bread, dole out the soup, shake the mattresses—in short, that from their earliest years they had been preparing for the post of Stubendienst. She agreed on the spot to make them her assistants.

The Falks therefore distribute the soup and cut our bread.

But it seems all that was only a timid beginning. Since the quarantine was lifted they have made such great strides that now they only steal our bread out of simple habit.

Their bed is a veritable bazaar. They were the ones who first traded in toothbrushes, needles, and soap. From morning till evening two of them conduct business. The third guards the kitty and takes care of little operations inside. Thus occupied, they cut our bread so distractedly and are so late distributing the soup that we're constantly in a state of rage and on the verge of a riot.

"Well," says Suri (age thirteen) indifferently, "we don't have a head for that."

And in the evening after a full day of plunder, lying broken with fatigue on their mattress, they're still busy making plans and consulting feverishly half the night; even in their sleep, they haggle or do accounts in Yiddish.

"Look at them," Sophie says to me. "I'll bet that two weeks from now they'll be living like the Poles, and maybe better."

"They have a sense of survival," I say. "Just look at their hands—short, powerful, and grasping, like birds of prey."

Let's move to the bed on the right. There it's "Madame," with her puny daughter. One day I called her "auntie" and she had a fit. Sophie and I are fully informed as to how many dinner services she had, of enamel, crystal, and Rosenthal china; the name of her dressmaker; the tips she was in the habit of leaving; and what she served when she entertained her daughter's friends, from the mushroom omelet to the almond-and-raisin cake.

Is the camp really made up of caricatures, or are they just the only ones you notice? The others, the *humans*, don't make waves, and live as unobtrusively as possible, as if on tiptoe.

Like our neighbor on the left, Illus from Miskolc. She moves little, and cautiously, like a night nurse in a hospital ward; she eats without making any noise, she doesn't snore, she never licks the bottom of her bowl. She's one of the few who say hello or respond to your greeting. It was she who bought the first piece of soap from the Falks, for two rations of bread. For that

she fasted two days. We tried in vain to get her to
accept two slices of bread.

"No, thanks, excuse me," she said, blushing.

She's an incurable "civilian."

———

Two frantic days. I don't move, I don't talk. I'm trying
to get my journal up to date.

———

We're going to work. Félicie has just announced it.
Maybe tomorrow . . . I'm not ready yet.

———

Census according to profession. Can't say "school-
girl." Sophie claims that the Germans love specialists.
The question is what to specialize in. The choice is
huge, and we only have ten minutes to decide
whether we want to be dressmakers, nurses, dancers,
or typists.

Seated at the table that's been set up for the purpose, Félicie writes down our professions on sheets
and threatens—looking even more exhausted than
usual—to send us straight off to Buchenwald to the
gas chamber (this gas chamber is alternately located at
Auschwitz, Dachau, or Buchenwald, depending on
her mood) if we don't immediately confess who it was

that put down: Jüdin, Häftlinge, Hure, Hexe,[1] and Dolores del Rio.

She hands out death by gas too lightly, it seems to me. What would happen to her barracks, which is, after all, the basis of her material well-being, if she carried out her terrifying promises? Where would she get the zlotys for the purple sweater that makes her look like an off-duty riding instructor?

Ah, no! We're not all "Dolores del Rios." Far from it! Although it's true that it's only the Jewish sense of humor that helps us bear the rest. I don't know, my word, what becomes of Jews without humor—like my neighbor on the right, for example, who wrote on her sheet, "Profession: society woman (bachelor's degree)."

I exclaimed, "What sense does that make in a labor camp?"

"I can't lie, my dear. My golden rule is to tell the truth under all circumstances."

"Why not homemaker, or cook?"

"Society woman! They ought to know that!"

She gave us a withering look. We barely managed to get her daughter's sheet away from her: "Completed seventh grade at Our Lady of Zion. Studied piano in Budapest with Emma Lövi."

As for Sophie and me, here's what we put on our

[1] Jew, detainee, whore, witch.

sheets, a single word: mason. At first I was leaning toward cooking. But I had to admit that with half a barracks full of cooks already signed up, that wasn't a great idea. The Fritzes would wonder what sort of place Transylvania might be, where half the population did the cooking and the other half hauled pots, peeled vegetables, and so on.

"Masons . . ."

I'll let Sophie speak: "There's nothing more marvelous than a body with muscles taut from working. It's so sublime to relax after a day of tiring exercise, when you finally savor repose in every fiber of your body."

I wonder where she gets her energy, on the four ounces of bread doled out by the Falks. I have nothing against exercise, as far as that goes! The open air! At Plaszow, nature is represented by a bare, gray hill. But even behind a gray hill the sun sets majestically, after pausing for a second on the summit like an orange on a roof. Sophie, who thinks there may be a quarry on the hill, is already sorry that we didn't choose "stonecutter" as our profession.

"You don't know," she says, "what a feeling it is to attack a formless and unyielding mass with a hammer, and see it take shape under your blows."

It's true that I don't know. But Sophie's enthusiasm hardly seems better founded! Except that she was once neighbors with a marble worker, who one day let her touch (she says "polish") a block of stone with a hammer.

Who would have thought the soul of a stonecutter slumbered in this consummate "theoretician"?

—

Hooray for the quarry!

I'd laugh if I had the strength. Sophie isn't laughing either.

She dragged along silently at my side on the way back; she didn't even have time to get into her bunk—sleep struck her down in a crouch. I haven't been able to close my eyes, I'm so stiff. How will I manage to decipher this scrawl? Yet I'm writing. What else can I do, the only one awake in this barracks full of "apoplectics"?

Thoughts of Egypt and other "labor camps" since before the Flood . . . Where do we get the idea that we're the *first?* We only repeat, always and endlessly . . .

Here, now, we're repeating the Bible.

"Torment." "Burning sun." The fact that I used those words before today seems unbelievable, frivolous. If wasted words had a voice, what a fuss they'd make! "What right do you have to use us lightly?" Here we earn the "right" to one or two every day.

And now I have a right to "torment" and "burning sun." I'm just a child, but I have a right to words that would make generations of elders turn pale.

I therefore wear that right with a sad pride.

Félicie—who is usually an hour early—went back to sleep, lost her memory, lost her mind, or something!

In any case the *Bergkapos*, three rather good-looking brutes, arrived before the Blockälteste did, when she finally showed up, we were already out of bed.

It all happened without pleas or threats, so quickly that the late arrival could hardly believe her eyes. We just had to see those Zorros, the way they walked, the way they held their riding crops, the ease and pleasure with which they used them, and upsy-daisy! (It took you, dear Félicie, a good five minutes to wake us.) These are pros! I had already noticed them at roll call, dressed in tight leather from head to foot like motorcycle riders.

"They must be stuffed," remarked Sophie.

They didn't even have to get close to the bunks before we tumbled out of bed, all groggy with sleep, half naked. They laughed when they saw Félicie, with their teeth that could chomp a mountain. The order hadn't even been given, and already the ranks had formed. And off we went. In a moment of inspiration Félicie jumped on us to count us, but a Kapo immediately swept her out of the way with a small movement of his elbow. By the time the poor girl got herself together, we were already out the gate of the enclosure.

We marched in step through the deserted camp, refreshed by the morning air, the exercise, and the excitement, alongside the young Kapo who had just cut short Félicie's enthusiasm. I watched him surreptitiously.

His face was not unfamiliar. He had already intrigued me from a distance, in the Appelplatz. Impossible to tell whether he was really awake behind his nearly closed eyelids. He seemed to be asleep at roll call, he swept Félicie out of the way in his sleep, he was sleeping as he walked, and at times he seemed to be enjoying a dream.

"Jurek!"

He didn't flinch, although the whole column turned around and the other Kapo—an energetic sort whose name (Johnny) suits him as well as do the riding crop, the leather shorts, and the brush-cut hair—came up laughing.

Johnny was already behind him when Jurek finally deigned to turn around, slowly. He listened with his eyes closed. Then he roared with laughter and turned his back. Johnny spoke in Polish, but everyone knew what it was about.

When the hill had first come into view, it had become obvious that the two thousand "cooks," "dress-

makers," and "pot carriers" were on their way toward
"nature," so to speak. A great uneasiness ran through
the ranks. People asked questions and became agitated. Johnny intervened with his riding crop; that's
how he learned from one of the "cooks" that there
had been a census in the barracks, according to *profession.* But how could you exercise the profession of
Hungarian-Romanian chef on a little knoll?

"They made up lists? Hmmm, hmmm," said
Johnny.

He burst out laughing and hurried off to regale his
colleagues.

If the absurdity of those *lists* should bother you, I'd
say to you that there's something worse than not understanding the Fritzes: *trying* to understand them!

"Look," said Sophie the stonecutter when we finally stopped in front of a sort of yellowish cliff from
which two Hungarians with picks were cutting
chunks. Quite a pile awaited us. We looked around for
the hammers.

But Johnny interrupted our daydreams with his
whistle. A strident and prolonged sound, ominous,
and then the riding crop struck and the torment began, and the terrible word: "Los! Los!"[1]

The blows rained down. I still have a mark on my
forehead, Sophie on the back of her neck.

[1] Move! Move!

Our job? To pass stones from hand to hand from one end of the hill to the other. Stones, exercise, the open air—it was all there!

Conclusion: Avoid *nature* as well as the Fritzes when you're "concentrated."

At times we dragged real blocks that we could barely lift. At other times we passed along ridiculous little rocks, almost pebbles. One Kapo for every twenty detainees; we didn't get a moment's respite, even when our tormentor was looking the other way, because if the chain stopped, another Kapo started hollering. They seemed almost as cornered as we were! SS were posted behind them, and even they didn't seem to be under any less pressure; they yelped constantly: "Der Kommandant kommt, halt fest die Hunde!"[1] In the end the distinguished visitor was impolite enough not to appear, but the torment didn't diminish because of it.

Anyone who had never seen "raw nerves" had only to look at the stripes on our naked backs.

No break for lunch. And for good reason: no lunch.

And yet that wasn't what was *unbearable*.

It was . . . the sun!

"Let's imagine we're in Africa, that we're blacks," I said.

"Why not pot roasts?" retorted Sophie.

[1] The commandant's coming, hold on to the dogs!

She turned toward me, and indeed I could have been looking at a big, sizzling roast. She was just as surprised, because I had turned a grayish-black; I was only a shade different from an Abyssinian.

But that exchange took place early, at the beginning of the morning. By midday our voices had been silenced by thirst. Many times I caught myself raising my head, which felt as if it was swelling constantly like a tire, toward the Kapo above.

"Are you crazy, or what? That's enough!"

And yet the stones and the hands continued to move, and always that "Los! Los!" And everything spun dizzily in my head. "The sun worshipers," I said to myself, "were actually people who *feared* the sun. And if this goes on, I'll either collapse or fall into some unknown religion."

It was as if years, a whole lifetime, had gone by since five by five we climbed toward that calvary.

Everything that had gone before—the bed, the bread distribution, my journal, school, my childhood—seemed like just a void, as if my life had begun on that hill and would very slowly end there, after thousands of years, when that accursed cliff was finally gone. And yet I didn't collapse. Each movement was a new torture, a new surprise. It was no longer I that moved, but something in me and with me. Through my lethargy I could see the hands, the stones, the Kapos pitching as if they were drunk. I, too, was pitching. One thought, always the same: *I can't do any more*, or *I'm going to faint* . . . But my hand continued to reach out, my back continued to bend.

What is this blasted *you must* that watches over me and sets me back up every time I'm ready to topple?

—

Jurek is on sentry duty here, leaning against a tree barely a yard from the ditch where I'm lying on my stomach like a saboteur. The brush hides me. But if the wind should move it aside, or if Jurek should decide to step over it . . . then God help me! But it doesn't occur to him. Maybe he's "playing hooky," too. Treating himself to a little solitude. A lonely torturer.

His muscular neck and heavy head lean against the tree; his gray eyes, wide open, stare straight ahead without blinking. They look like two gaping holes (maybe he's right to hide them).

A wild animal at rest. A melancholy, inscrutable animal.

If I wanted to, I could write a thousand times in a row: *brute, brute, brute* . . .

The riding crop hangs inert in his rather languid hand. It could be the hand of a doctor, a designer . . .

I try to imagine what he might have been like before the war. A civilian Jurek! But he was never a
"civilian," just a little boy. This is where he grew up.
This is where he became Jurek.

Watching someone who thinks he's alone! A mad
adventure!

Suppose I suddenly popped up: "Peek-a-boo!"

—

A fifteen-minute break. The woman supervisor has
arrived. (The only Boche who has never raised a hand
against anyone.)

She's often surrounded by the three Bergkapos.
That's why I'm not too surprised to see her approach
with a pack of cigarettes. She sticks one in Jurek's
mouth, gives him a light, and lights one for herself. As
she does, she giggles constantly. Jurek doesn't seem
surprised either; he looks at her, friendly behind his
again-lowered eyelids, as if nothing were more normal
than to be here together, smoking.

"Has anyone been looking for me?" Jurek suddenly
asks.

"Just me," says the supervisor. (And she starts
laughing again, as if someone were tickling her.)

"Hush," says Jurek.

And suddenly I'm dumbfounded: He grabs her by
the shoulders, pulls her to him, and no, he doesn't

kiss her, but says to her as he holds her, "Go away, Liese, go away."

"Are you scared?" asks the supervisor, looking at him in an amused way.

"Yes," Jurek answers dryly.

She shrugs her shoulders, makes a face, and turns on her heel.

She's hardly gone any distance when Jurek calls to her, so softly that I can barely hear him.

"Liese!"

She turns around at once. She takes a few steps, then starts running toward him. They fall into each other's arms.

Love! I know something about it (there are several movie theaters in our town). Even so, I don't see why they bite each other so furiously, looking so gloomy. They look like two people waging a life-and-death struggle in their sleep.

Jurek is the first to pull away.

"Go away, go away," he says to her in a funny, hoarse voice.

He doesn't look very well, and watches her impatiently. The German, on the other hand, looks as radiant as if she had just been given a medal in front of God and the Reich.

Now that they're standing up straight, next to each other, I see that she's half a head taller than Jurek.

She leaves. Jurek walks back and forth, cracking his whip, his face stern. One time he stops so close to my hiding place that if he moved his foot forward a little bit, it would touch me. Then suddenly he turns on his heel and leaves. Phew!

———

My hiding place . . . I came across it by accident.

I was thirsty, and I was staggering as I passed the stones; I tried to swallow my saliva, but I had almost none left.

Red circles danced before my eyes. "Sunstroke, and that's that," I said to myself. I had only one thought: to sneak off in a corner, somewhere in the shade.

The johns aren't far away, but the Germans and the Kapos pay particular attention to them. When a crowd gathers, you find yourself getting a shower of rocks. It's not unusual for them to show up in person, or for their riding crops to catch you in a delicate position. Then you take flight with your clothes in a disorder that's easy to imagine and that delights the Fritzes and the Kapos.

All in all, sunstroke is preferable to a cracked head. It took me a long time to make up my mind, but at midday our people began to pass out; I was still on my

feet and in no danger of losing my merry consciousness.

I had my chance when I saw the guard heading
toward the johns; I started running in the opposite
direction. It was obvious that the farther I got from
the chain, the better off I'd be. I had to stop suddenly
at a ditch that blocked my way. I jumped without
thinking. I stayed for a good while in a crouch, holding my breath. I heard only silence.

My legs went to sleep, but I didn't dare stretch
them out. It took me an hour or more to calm down.
On the hill everything kept going, the chain, the
Fritzes, their dogs, the whole routine!

As I lay there on my stomach, it all reached me in
the form of a continuous hum, mechanical and almost
inoffensive.

Then my attention was drawn to a different noise,
silvery and regular, as if farther up the ditch, in the
ground, a watch was ticking.

I had to crawl barely a yard, and only my guardian
angel kept me from crying out; at the bottom of the
ditch, among the pebbles, water was gushing. I had
found a spring. Then I was nothing but throat, skin,
and "thankfulness" (another word I have a *right* to).

When I saw the chain disperse, I returned to it as
easily as I had left. No one had been looking for me.
No one had noticed that there was one shaven head

gone. What's nice about this place is that no one misses you.

Since then I go to my "office" every morning. I have my "system": I take my place at the end of the chain, and I leave it dragging a big stone and looking determined, as if I had a special order to carry out. Sometimes I even snarl as I go: "Make way, please, make way." I spend the midday break on the hill with the others. Sophie hardly finds this behavior reassuring; she doesn't dare take the risk.

I don't either; I'm not going to risk losing one second of solitude.

—

Everything is going better since I've been writing during the day, except for the few minutes' walk in the morning with my notebook in the bread bag that I wear bandolier style like everyone else; taking it out of the camp is certainly less of a risk than leaving it in my mattress at the mercy of the Stubendiensts, who poke into everything, and the dwarf's special commandos. Unlikely that we'll be searched on our way. Yet as I approach the gate I feel an odd emptiness where my neck should be. There are times when I detest the notebook and feel "harnessed" to it as if to an infernal chariot. Three times I've missed the extra food. Twice it was soup and once it was jam.

"What are you complaining about?" says Sophie. "You're the only one who isn't working for the Fritzes."

—

I can hear the beating of my heart. Like a separate thing, cowering in the bushes.

Barely half an hour ago a white horse jumped over me. Its glistening, muscular belly trembled with the effort, because the burden it was carrying was hardly an ordinary one. The last time I saw such a mass of flesh was at the circus, and it was carrying a motorcycle and rider on each shoulder.

Everything started out so well! As we left, a few broken clouds floated in the sky and a nice cool wind promised an end to the dog days. Besides that, two pleasant pieces of news: They were going to distribute two pails of jam in each barracks, and the German *Bergkommando* had undergone a complicated dental operation, and his aching gums kept him from yelling. He had been gargling all morning, a demijohn in his hand, and Johnny was entertaining him with anecdotes because from time to time, with his mouth closed and twisted in pain, he would puff up with laughter.

The whole time, the stones passed smoothly from hand to hand. The rhythm made me lazy. Instead of

writing I looked around constantly, until at last I recognized the girl in uniform. She was carrying a helmet
in her hand; she stood leaning against the Kapos'
bunker, and from a distance she resembled a sapling.
I could only half see Jurek (the ground slopes in front
of the bunker), his zippered jacket of dark green
leather. His eyes were closed and he was barely moving his lips, as if talking made him tired.

In less than a second, everything changed. The supervisor's carefree face, round and happy, became
suddenly sharp and almost unpleasant with concentration. Narrowing her eyes, she peered at a spot in the
valley. Then she took Jurek by the shoulders and
turned him around. Johnny and the Bergkommando
had already joined them.

Four pairs of eyes, four sharp faces were fixed on
the same spot.

Not a word was spoken, and yet the chain stopped,
each person with a stone in her hand. Fear! It seems
to propagate by waves, like sound.

From where our group was, they couldn't see the
valley; they could see only the four tight, attentive
faces.

The aching jaws started to bellow: "Los, Schweine,
bewegt euch!"[1] And the dance began. Saint Vitus's
dance.

[1] Come on, you pigs, move it!

Alone in my hiding place, I heard the branches quiver and the ground shake. I thought it was an earthquake before I made out the sound of galloping. I barely had time to flatten myself out when the white belly was already flying over me, followed by other bellies. Then they must have stopped. I didn't hear anything but my own terrified breathing.

The man on the white horse was there where Liese had been standing shortly before. A panting whale, with an enormous belly and fat, pendulous breasts. Numerous medals trembled on his chest. So this was the famous cannibal aesthete! His head reminded me of a smooth, naked ass. How could those swollen paws hold a revolver? How could decisions emerge from above that triple chin? How could cruelty, perversity, or any other "trait" penetrate that obscene layer of fat? Was it believable that this shapeless mass could be anything more than a lazy metabolism, that it could want anything other than to digest, to catch its breath, to preserve its huge organism from apoplexy? No matter how long I looked at it, it expressed nothing but obesity.

A gray bulldog gamboled at his feet. It was the only creature that dared to move.

But what's wrong? A sound, neither human nor animal, raucous and persistent . . . Still the "face" remained motionless and serene. I wondered whether the bizarre sound was coming from him or from his mount . . .

Suddenly he spurred his horse to a gallop. He brought his riding crop down on someone's back. Frightened, the poor girl must have dropped the stone she was carrying on the horse's hoof, because the animal reared and the strange sound began again. Now I saw a sign that he was angry: The triple chin trembled.

"Rex, komm her,"[1] he called to his dog, indicating the girl.

And the chase began.

She jumped over the ditch, first tried to hide behind the bunker, and then plunged toward the valley.

She tripped and had to abandon her shoes.

She was still holding her own, but she stumbled often and started to panic.

The bulldog was calmer. His superiority was obvious; he's a "pro."

I didn't see them anymore.

The stones continued to pass between trembling hands. The rider was behind, watching from very close, motionless, with a jovial, almost paternal expression above his three chins, as if to say "May God bless you, my children."

Finally the bulldog reappeared: alone. In his big

[1] Rex, come here!

eyes, dim with satiety and fatigue, lay the indifference of the well fed. He belched.

The riders went on their way immediately, as if they had only been waiting for him to return.

Johnny brought back the body (or what was left of it) in his arms.

It was unrecognizable. But the bunk on the left is empty, the one that belonged to Illus from Miskolc. It won't be long before the Falks' bazaar expands there.

I wonder whether there exists anywhere else a place like this, where God the Father is taken to task almost constantly. If He created Illus in His image, then the same is true of her killer. Madame, who adopted Christianity in the hope of saving her daughter, no longer knows what saint to pray to. She's certain of only one thing: "All this cannot be the work of men."

"That leaves the devil," I suggest.

She has her doubts, but when you think about it, isn't he the only one you would suspect in this place?

I, who even have doubts about my doubts, now pray only to my breath: "Don't abandon me, please."

—

Well, I forgot my bread bag with my notebook on the bunk. I had barely arrived on the hill when the downpour started. Needless to add that my rag of a bag would not have stopped my "work" from dissolving.

Even in my sleep I think about it, I search for it under the mattress. And today (what day is this?) I *forgot* it!

I got as far as the main gate without suspecting a thing. Only then did a reflexive anxiety make me remember it. If I had forgotten my arms, I couldn't have been any more stunned.

———

For a change of pace, we're "ditchdiggers" in a hailstorm! They cut clods of various sizes from the side of the hill that we're supposed to flatten with shovels, over an area so big that we can only laugh, like one-armed men who've been ordered to swim across the Danube. The Kapos themselves can't deny that this new "job," like the one with the chain, has no other purpose than to keep us "occupied." The best proof is that they make us work in the middle of a storm, when the ground is sticky and we can't flatten anything but mud, and then only during the rare moments when our balance isn't threatened by the gusts of wind and the flying ice doesn't force us to close our eyes. Leaning on our shovels, we search blindly for the next person's hand. The blind leading the blind. Holding on to one another, we make a rampart of our bodies against the wind—to the great annoyance of the Kapos, who can't do the same. Stumbling among the puddles, slipping and swearing, they wait for the order to quit.

They wait in vain.

During a moment of calm, I raise my eyes and see something really funny—a sort of gigantic bird soaring on the mist! It takes me some time to realize that its "wings" are our tattered clothes, and that this flying monster is us.

"Why are you whining? We're as wet as you are," growl the Kapos, huddling in their leather clothes.

Then no one growls anymore; it's the storm that's in command. It shakes us, trying to decide whether to knock us to the ground or throw us into the valley. And this is just an innocent game. When it really gets going, it covers us entirely. Everything is now just a vicious wave, and only one thing matters: air. We struggle for breath, huddled against one another, using our bodies as a barrier against the storm.

How did it happen? I don't know. But suddenly I found myself alone, sitting in a puddle—or rather a stream—of mud; waves of mud propelled by the storm swept me along like a pebble. It was impossible to get any footing on the slippery ground; the wind knocked me back down at once. How long did the slide last? When I was finally able to stop and stand up, I was well down in the valley and could only see the hill from afar, a disturbing distance away.

What if in the meantime the order came to quit! The whole group would be stuck there in the storm waiting for me! I have a piece of ice in my chest. But even if it's frozen, my heart must be beating, because dead people don't feel the cold. From somewhere out of the depths of my terror looms the wet Appelplatz and the post . . .

Suddenly I hear voices behind me. Maybe I'm not the only one who slid; or maybe they're coming to look for me! I turn around: nobody. The voices are coming from a barracks a few paces behind me. Women's voices, it seems to me as I get closer, but I can't make out the words; at the door my courage fails me and I stand there hesitating until another gust of wind decides for me.

When I open the door I'm engulfed and almost blinded by hot steam; from the noise of the shower I know I'm in a Waschraum. After the thousands of nudists I've rubbed elbows with, here I am stupefied by a handful of naked women! Is it their hair? Incredible curves covered with lather, soaping their perfumed skin, others rubbing themselves with Turkish towels. My bare skull, my tattered clothes, and this smell of cold cream! I'd like to leave before anyone notices me. Instead, I rip a piece from my dress and make myself a scarf. I could die, with this wet rag on my head! I want to be back outside with my group, somewhere in the storm!

Nevertheless I don't move, frozen like a statue on the threshold, praying quietly that I won't be noticed.

Someone pushes me, I stumble, I bump against the door; the woman who has come in with a blast of wind didn't see me. I sink down onto a "hole." I sob. I've never had such a bitter need to.

A hand brushes me, unties the soaked rag on my head. Through my sobs I can't understand what she's saying, but it doesn't matter because the drenched scarecrow that I am is being caressed—which verges on the fantastic in this place, and plunges me into a kind of happiness that's as fragile as a hallucination. I continue to sniffle, but it's as a precaution. To keep her there. She sits down on the "hole" beside me and tells me not to be embarrassed, that crying does you good; it's something that she has lost, alas, and doesn't think she'll ever get back. After that everything vanishes: the storm, the hill, the others, even my anxieties and the post. I talk, I can't stop—about my parents, my class, my journal, my determination to survive. (Someone to listen, that's as rare here as caresses.) I interrupt myself suddenly, with the feeling that I've been left alone. But she's there, smiling at me, although as if from a distance, with that omniscient Polish smile that

I've learned to distrust. (They think of us as harmless lunatics, whom it's better not to contradict.)

She isn't going to bore me with her story. Things are all right now. She and her husband run the locksmith shop. And yet she'd trade places with me on the spot, just as I am, soaked and ragged. She stands up, wrapping a towel around her hair.

"She's going away!" I say to myself, distressed.

"Tell me, tell me what's happening!"

And at once I feel out of place, clingy, and I hush. As she dries her hair she continues to smile at me, telling me that one should never lose hope—all the things that people tell children, who are almost always less stupid than people think they are. She asks me to wait a second, she wants to bring me something.

She takes a long time, and while I wait my imagination, inflamed by hunger, has time to conjure up a roast chicken, to fantasize at will.

When she appears with some clothes over her arm, I'm almost disappointed. But that only lasts a second. A black lamé blouse—no, don't put it on right away, first let's try this sweater. (If I put it on over my dress, the Germans might confiscate it from me.) Under the sweater the blouse looks nicer, and I also get a silk scarf, a white one! With her slim hands she wraps it as a turban. It goes marvelously with my dark skin and the black blouse!

"My, you look sweet!" she cries, kissing me on both cheeks.

Was it really she who a few minutes ago was smiling at me in such a devastated way? Was it I who was sobbing so bitterly in her arms? (You can't even depend on your own sorrows!)

Several pocket mirrors are held out to me. But the window is still the best; bare arms push me toward it.

All the bathers are amazed and delighted along with me. I seem to have forgotten myself completely. Is it really me, this turbaned youngster, all spiffy and new?

Before she goes away she tells me her name again: Elli Reich. I can find her every morning a few hundred yards from there, at the locksmith shop. She hugs me, grateful, it seems, for the pleasure that she's gotten from comforting me. In my excitement I haven't even noticed that the storm has stopped, as if intimidated by my surprising appearance.

I arrive just at the midday break. The ditchdiggers are soaked to the bone, which doesn't stop them from staring with eyes as big as wardrobe mirrors. Wherever I turn, I see my shocking reflection: all the filthy things I must have been up to, to extort this "loot" from a lecherous old Pole. I know the truth will never do, because nothing gets past the law of the camp: "You don't get something for nothing." It's easier to believe that a "lecherous man infatuated by my charms" is taking care of me! Ruchele, who distributes the soup, gets flustered to the point that she serves me first. Sophie, who looks like a half-drowned mouse, says between two sneezes, "You got those things and it doesn't matter how!" That's all she can find to say.

"Woher hast du die Sache?"

"Von einer Polin."[1]

I hear this funny voice—mine—as if it were coming from someone else's throat. Jurek, out of nowhere, is watching me from under his eyelids.

"Ganz nett,"[2] he says through his teeth, and disappears.

———

A half hour of sleep would fix me up. But it's hopeless in the barracks; Sunday is wash day. Everybody's running around excitedly, bundled up in blankets from which nothing emerges but pointed shoulders, shaven heads, and an incessant chatter that's enough to give you a migraine. Clothes are hung out as far as the eye can see, and with their spots, their rips, and especially their rank odor (cold water doesn't take it out), they brighten and stink up our day of rest. Since I can't

[1] Where did you get those things?
From a Polish woman.
[2] Not bad.

write, I follow the "exploits" of our new neighbor on the left, who spends her leisure time worrying a piece of clay (the clay is actually mud that she "fortifies" with sand). She turns it into funny shapes, shapes you don't see in nature, as if the natural world disturbed her. It's true that nature hasn't been very kind to her, decking her out with a mustache that raises doubts as to her sex.

She says, "It's not my problem." At the moment she seems to be concentrating, distant, as if she's planning a major work, but then she turns and gravely says, "Okay."

She was considering the price of a piece of soap that the Falks were offering her in exchange for a whole week's marmalade.

—

If only I didn't owe everything to my luck!

I've barely reached the bath hut, where I wanted to ask about the locksmith shop, and I haven't even had time to catch my breath when a shaven head runs up to me, panting:

"Jurek's looking everywhere for you. If we don't come up with you in five minutes, he's going to kill the whole bunch.

"What are you waiting for? Are you deaf?"

She grabs me. I let myself be dragged off. We fly

over the hill, I feel weightless. My brain is empty, my hand in hers is soft as putty. She lets go of me when we get to the Kapos' bunker. When I enter, Jurek has his back turned. He's rummaging in a box or a bag. It's impossible for him not to have heard the door. I have time to catch my breath. I step forward. He doesn't move. For a moment I stand there, looking at his back. This is his way of playing on my fear. He's doing it consciously. He's enjoying this, the beast!

"You wanted to see me?"

I take a step toward him and he turns around. I notice, not without a touch of pleasure, that he has to clear his throat.

"Where did you go?" he asks in a very low voice that gives me the shivers.

But my voice doesn't let anything show, thank God. I stand up straight: "To the bathroom. I was indisposed."

"Indisposed how?"

"Diarrhea."

I think the worst is over, and I stare at him without batting an eye. The look on his face chills me again.

"We'll see," he hisses, grabbing my wrist as if to take my pulse.

I pull my hand back, with a movement that's no more intentional than the blinking of an eye from a speck of dust.

The hand that grabbed mine hangs there for a moment. I mutter, "Ich habe kein Fieber."

"Aber eine Ohrfeige, die hast du."[1]

And with that I feel something heavy, a millstone, hit my skull. The bunker tilts, and everything goes dark; only afterward does my cheek begin to burn.

I try to hold myself straight as I leave. I've reached the door when he flings after me: "Wait!"

I hear his muffled voice at my back: "Where are the things you had on yesterday?"

"Go to hell," I say, turning around.

He just laughs nastily. He seems to enjoy the rage he inspires as much as the fear. In any case, I leave the bunker on my feet, with the scarlet imprint of his paw on my cheek.

I work my shovel until evening wearing that mark, heedless of the chatter, the jokes, and even the sun.

I just remember one piece of advice that I received, but not who gave it to me: "Better to avoid these butchers."

To which I responded, "I'm going to kill him . . . with a brick."

[1] I haven't got a fever.
But you do get a slap.

—

Ditchdigging! We drag our shovels around without using them. The heat, staying on your feet—nothing is as exhausting as the absurdity of it all. The waste of precious hours drags on me like a ball and chain. It's like one of those tedious dreams where all sorts of insignificant, pointless, and yet tiring little things happen. You get bored in your sleep, you know it all isn't possible and that you need to wake up; and at the very moment when after a painful effort you almost make it to the threshold of consciousness, some new nonsense takes you away once more. And yet today was not one of the worst, because of the almost inconceivable *event* that happened.

The midday break was over. We were about to take up our shovels again when we saw a strange group coming up toward the bunker. They were shaven— the colorful scarves and the clean clothes couldn't hide that. Leading them was a slim but not emaciated girl in a green dress that was attractive—if a little short—with an armband on the sleeve: Lagerkapo. Good grief, that had never before been seen among the shaven heads! Her poised walk, her nonchalant bearing, and finally the unmistakable "pillars" visible below her short dress: It was indeed the "prodigy," Juliette, radiant and almost pretty. (I was sure that she and her mother had escaped from the hill by becoming Stubendiensts.) There she was shaking Johnny's hand, talking seriously as if important things were going on.

The group of women waited a certain distance away.

Intimidated by their great cleanliness, we didn't even think of approaching them. As for the "prodigy," I was hardly surprised. Isn't the extraordinary routine for her? I wouldn't have been all that astonished if she had suddenly drawn a dagger and stabbed the Bergkommando, à la Charlotte Corday.

Overwhelmed by the great event, I almost forgot: an assassination attempt on the Führer. The new guard (a German from Transylvania) told us. He takes advantage of the slightest lull—for example, when the Bergkommando is yelling from the other side of the hill—to tell us wonderful tall tales in our own language.

According to him, the war is as good as over, finished, *schluss*[1] (you wonder why we're here, and why he carries his rifle and glances so nervously left and right).

It wasn't some terrorist, but a pure-blooded German commander who carried out the attempt. He made a mess of it. He richly deserved the bullet that

[1] At an end, over with.

he got; in the course of such a long war he should have learned to aim, at the very least.

That being said, I myself have moments of amnesia when I don't understand what I'm doing there dragging a shovel. I look around bewildered. According to Sophie, I have a dangerous tendency to relapse into logic.

—

"Solidarity" (you usually run into it in war novels). I ran into it today, here at Plaszow, in the course of this day that God made stifling.

How diligently our "friends" rack their brains to find ways to get more "exercise" into our lives! And they're constantly "finding" things: Today, for example, it's "piece work." Everyone has to flatten a certain area of ground. Those who don't finish will do so during the midday break. Those for whom that's not enough time, well, they'll see what happens! The "piece" is perhaps not excessive, but as exhausted as I am, it's out of the question. Everyone has passed me. I can only see their backs; the farthest away is the sculptress's. Just watching her makes me tired. What zeal! You'd think she enjoys it. She hums (with that mustache!), she works in bursts! I see her coming back to my area after having finished her piece; I motion to her.

"Keep quiet," she says.

I can't believe my eyes, I drag myself over to her.

"Don't worry about it, I've already finished my piece."

I must have an idiotic look on my face. She smiles.

Last night she heard me talking out loud. "She's dreaming," she said to herself. But no! With my head against the partition I was working, and as if my hand wasn't able to keep up with my thoughts, I was murmuring impatiently, dictating to myself, gesticulating, grimacing, a real show! From her bag she took out a clay head as big as a fist, lined with wrinkles, the mouth half open and the expression tormented—the head of an old woman.

She guessed what I was thinking, and said that she had a terrible time modeling me because my expression changed constantly along with my thoughts, but that she was planning to make a new head of me, at rest, with my pretty turban. She makes plans and organizes things as if the camp were a workshop, just another outlet for her overflowing energy.

As she helps me with my "piece," she tells me that I mustn't kill myself at the job. She's used to physical work, thanks to her trade and her peasant origins. (Jewish peasants—I didn't know such a thing existed.) She has also been in prison.

She waits for me to catch up before she explains. They loaded up the Jews in the prisons with no exceptions, no distinction—three months or twenty years, it was all the same.

"Which means that this place is the end of the line?"

"We're in the open air," she says. "In prison we didn't get walks, or visits."

I wonder what offense she might have committed, with her energy. But she didn't "commit" anything except leaflets and speeches against the established order. I happen to be the daughter of a lawyer, and I know that to shake up the established order you need to have the army on your side, the police, the legal system . . . and that there are "jokers" who think they can do it with leaflets. There was a couple who lived in the same apartment building that we did. Sometimes the man and sometimes the woman was in prison; when one of them was free and came to talk to my father, we children were forbidden to come in. They were serious and secretive people. The principles for which they endured horrifying things made me shudder with respect, because I'm one of those people who tremble at the dentist's.

I must have a funny look on my face, because she says, "Forget it, if it bothers you."

I say that she's right to talk about it, because wherever we're from and whoever we are, we can't be any more locked up than we are now.

"Which won't stop you from writing tonight, I'll bet."

"Or stop you from wanting to change the world without one lousy bomb or even a pistol."

She laughs. "More than ever! At the risk of becoming a comic character in your journal."

"My journal and your leaflets amount to about the same thing. They're both laughable."

But I don't think she's a comic character; they never laugh at themselves.

—

The Bergkapos are amusing themselves by using reptiles for whips. A snake smacks my shoulder. It's Jurek's idea of a joke. I don't give him the pleasure of making one of those shrill, "typically female" sounds with which the hill resounds. He spins the thing around his head, which seems like quite a performance for a dead reptile. It stands straight up in the air, in the middle of the giggling ditchdiggers (who are transported with delight). With his way of watching from under closed eyelids, his tight mask, and his lithe walk, he reminds you of a magician, a juggler—in short, a circus performer. He plunges his hand into his pocket, pulls out a little box in pink wrapping, and shoves it into my hand.

"Mach es nur auf."[1] It's an order.

To avoid having a mouse or a toad jump in my face, I hold the box away from me and open it carefully. What comes out is neither a mouse nor a toad, but a strong odor of sardines. I'm holding a sardine-and-butter sandwich. I don't look over at the "mask," but I can feel that it's tense. I can also feel the waves of hunger coming toward me from all around. I'm at the center of all the empty bellies, all the starvation in this world. Watch out, I say to myself, above all don't be too hasty. I close the box and toss it calmly (although I wish it had landed farther away). I watch the crowd run and throw themselves on it, and Jurek, his face dark, rushes into the melee. Finally, with the usual three fingers in his mouth, Johnny sounds his siren. Everyone's in place, and we start walking.

The walk seems very long to me because of my mood of pent-up jubilation; I'm expecting that once I'm on my mattress the happiness will finally explode and overwhelm me. But nothing! I've noticed it before: The joys on which I count too much don't materialize; it's as if I had won a race and noticed at the end that I'd been running all alone, with no competition and no supporters.

[1] Open it.

P.S.: An impulse: While Sophie went to get the bread, I got dressed up in my new things—after which, under the blanket, I got undressed and stuffed everything into the mattress. What was the sense of that? Who knows!

If you could manage to understand yourself, you could work things out with other people . . . maybe.

—

I'm writing on an overturned box, sitting on a stool. Between my head and the unbearable sky of Plaszow is a bunch of ceiling beams (from underneath, with my eyes half closed, they look like they're floating). I keep watching them, as if they might vanish from one moment to the next. But I'm not "playing hooky." This is my *legal* roof. I'm an *employee* in an underwear storage depot.

Employee . . . it's enough to make you giddy, and as I write I wear a sort of permanent smile. The smile of someone who, in the winter, looks out from a warm, safe place at a world that's icy cold and filled with the unknown. Thinking about everything that I've escaped: the sun, the rain, the Kapos, the bare asses in the latrines running from the whip, Jurek . . .

This morning at roll call, my friend with the notebook made his appearance. He called for silence and

passed back and forth several times in front of the
column, peering at each rank, his long face tight with
attention. First he chose a "blond" girl, Alice, which
didn't surprise anyone. Out of two thousand heads,
there's only one that's plainly "blond." It's actually
just a matter of a fringe on her forehead, which the
Slovak barber spared after having worked the scissors
back and forth in a golden cascade. That's why this
female Samson is still with us; the fringe is more ef-
fective than all of the Falks' schemes. As a
Stubendienst, Alice has never missed her double ration of soup—nor has her cousin Magda, whom she
has managed to keep with her.

That made two who had already left the column,
and the man with the notebook looked carefully over
the ranks as if he was searching for someone. I felt my
heart in my throat. Nothing would have made me
happier than to step forward, but as in those nightmares where you can't move even though your life
depends on it, I didn't budge. Suddenly the blood
rushed to my head: Ruchi Falk was standing in front
of the Lagerkapo. Her phony, honeyed tone, her unspeakable vulgarity, her ugliness—none of that mat-
tered, her story won him over: Her sister is only
thirteen, a weak and sickly child, and the work on the
hill is killing her. A murmur ran through the column.
Surele had never gone to the hill! And now the little

obscenity was standing beside Alice and Magda. Four girls from Dunaszerdahely joined the group, and that was no accident either.

We Transylvanians were the most numerous in the transport. But what do numbers mean against the weight of a solid coalition? The impenetrable conspiracy of a gang from the same village? One for all and all for one. Like musketeers who are a little bit obtuse, and illiterate to the last man. The edge of the world—didn't you know?—is the Danube, and in particular the Danube at Dunaszerdahely. To them, everything else is just "stories." They have the good fortune of distrusting everything they're not familiar with, starting with the vocabulary that they merrily wreck; we call them the "Huns."

So that made seven, counting the Huns. The Lagerkapo counted them one more time and pierced the ranks with a concentrated look. Sophie pulled me, the sculptress pushed. I remained motionless while another me, anxious and eager, followed all his movements. Finally he turned to Félicie, disappointed.

"Wo ist die Kleine . . . die Kleine?"[1] he asked, and his eyes stopped not far from me.

"Aber ich bin gar nicht klein bitte."[2]

Finally I stood up straight and took a step forward,

---

[1] Where is the little . . . the little one?
[2] But I'm not at all little.

my face burning from all the eyes on me, the Lagerkapo looking relieved and annoyed at the same time.

"Warum hast du dich nicht sofort gemeldet?"[1]

I murmured that I didn't know, and suddenly I remembered Sophie.

"My best friend, please, take her in the group!"

Not possible, he only needed eight people. But those he would take care of.

As we were leaving we met the three Bergkapos. They were late. Or were we lined up early today? Jurek promptly spotted me and stopped in front of the Lagerkapo. They spoke in Polish, but I understood from their glances at me that Jurek must have explained to him that I was in his group, and the Lagerkapo looked him up and down, nonplussed (we're all in his group). He looked at me in a mildly curious way. He said that I could go back to the hill if I wanted to. I shook my head: No. Go back! Merciful God!

The hill! If only I could drive it from my nightmares. I preferred the Huns, who were already scowling at me, as if by refusing to go back I was imposing myself, occupying a spot they had a right to.

And this is the "store"! Imagine a very old trash can, festooned with spiderwebs and mold. You have to

---

[1] Why didn't you come forward right away?

rummage for a long time before you unearth, among these natural elements, a few pairs of men's underpants yellowed with age, and then as your eye adjusts, a quantity of women's underpants, undershirts, blouses, and sweaters thrown haphazardly or stuck to each other and smelling of mold. They must have had some color once. You can find traces of it under the thick layers of dust and dirt if you shake them. From time to time I decide to. I quickly turn away, coughing; I'm afraid of betraying thoughts that an *employee*, and especially a newcomer, can't afford. Because we, the newcomers, still have neither undershirts nor underpants. We buy every rag and every scrap of soap with our "ration." How many "rations" of bread lie here in the dust, half eaten by moths? That doesn't seem to bother our bosses, who are well-meaning, as far as that goes, and who stroll comfortably in their impeccable blouses among this garbage, in an odor of rats and mold. Every time they glance outside, they pull the spiderwebs back from the window like a curtain. This proves that they must have used curtains in their previous lives.

The oldest is Frau Ellis, a dry, worn-out, nervous person whose age is impossible to tell. And yet the "nervous" one is Sonia, who is younger—in her thirties, so she claims. She also says that we shouldn't take her too seriously. She fidgets constantly, rarely finishes her sentences, doesn't wait for an answer when she asks a question. Talking is just a tic, according to her, because who at Plaszow would have anything to say that hasn't already been said? The fact that she's alive this morning doesn't say anything about the evening, or an hour from now, since you can never know anything with those "dogs." She's right, repetition is fatal, even for a tragedy. If you've heard one, you've heard them all: the ghetto, the "actions," the futility of everything. And the word that they repeat endlessly: *Scheisse.*[1]

It was from her that we learned the story of the third and youngest of the storekeepers, Vania; she's an "Aryan," the only daughter of a rich farmer. She had the outlandish idea of marrying a Jew in the ghetto. She followed him to the camp although, through her family's intervention and for a large fee, the "dogs" were willing to release her if she agreed to a divorce. That was out of the question for Vania. Her husband was killed last year during an "action." Since then she walks up and down in the storeroom the whole blessed day and in the barracks all night. She's always been a sphinx, but now she never opens her mouth; she agrees ahead of time with everything, it doesn't matter what. "She only breathes out of habit," says Sonia, and maybe that's better for her. Apparently in-

[1] Shit.

difference preserves. She doesn't seem broken by her drama. On the contrary, she bears it wonderfully—with her huge, dark-circled eyes, her transparent skin, and her otherworldly air, she seems like a living illustration of her romantic story. It's hard to believe that as ethereal and tragic as she is, she feeds herself, gets up every morning, and flushes the toilet like everyone else. "She eats, anyway," remarks one of the Huns bluntly. "Otherwise she wouldn't have the strength to keep running all day long." "You need a thick skin," she adds, "to live in garbage. With all those dead and those stories behind her." She claims to have seen fat Sonia giving bread to the crows. "If I just knew German, I'd tell her that there are people here who are hungrier than either the crows or the dead."

Doesn't it ever occur to them to open the windows? And us? What are we here for, if not to clean up? Apparently the spiderwebs are their "decor." They've spent years accumulating all this mess, and they need to hold on to it; it's their past, their museum in a way. It's "period" filth; maybe if they removed it all they'd feel lost, homeless.

Interminable discussions. Finally we entrust the affair to Alice, because of her fringe, her resolute manner, and her excellent German. "I'm going to try," she says, "come what may."

And she plants herself squarely in front of Sonia:

"Please show us what our work consists of. We would like to get started."

Sonia's eyebrows go up to the roots of her hair; the question has taken her by surprise.

"Maybe you could clean the floor . . ." she says hesitantly.

"Clean the floor? What's the point of that, when the walls, the shelves, the windows, in fact everything, is caked with dirt?"

It's one of the Huns who blurts that out, backing it up with vigorous gestures. The point is emphatically restated by Alice, who knows how to handle herself. She may be from the same village or the same region, but she's from the upper crust. The Huns worship her madly, just as they detest me. Why? It doesn't matter, the Huns don't need reasons, they function automatically according to tribal impulses.

"You mean," Sonia asks worriedly, "that all this would be . . ." And with her short arm she describes a circle.

"That's right," I cry, "a complete housecleaning."

She seems to weigh the proposition, suddenly catches on, and starts clapping her hands.

"That's marvelous! That's perfect!"

And she gives me a big kiss on the cheek. I feel the barbarians' hate go through me like an arrow. Even so, we did a good job together. All we have left for tomorrow are the windows and the floor. We could have done more if our bosses hadn't been under our feet constantly. For the first time since I've been in the camp I moved purposefully. I even got something personal out of it: Using four packing crates, I set up a "work room" for myself in one corner.

We had a visit from the Lagerkapo. He pretended not to recognize the place. To please us he probably exaggerated his surprise. He offered us his hand. He started with me, and since I didn't understand right away, I was a little slow and very clumsy slipping my hand into his. Can you forget how to shake hands? This little nothing was enough to put me in a bad mood.

P.S.: His name is Konhauser, and he used to run a retirement home in Silesia. From there to the morgue, I thought, is just one step.

—

I'm hopeless. Filthy, stupid blunders are going to be the end of me. I'll never get past Dunaszerdahely, or my problems with it. And yet I had the key to the situation in my hand. One moment, one gesture, and the dreaded town would have opened to me. It was that unique moment and that gesture that I missed. I'm lost, suffering the massive resentment of a horde of half-wits. I can't even console myself by saying that it wasn't my fault, unless I can blame it on my personal demon (vanity personified), who whispers to me constantly, "Don't let yourself be taken advantage of." And I don't let myself be taken advantage of! And I pay and I keep paying! And it doesn't stop! Today "he" used Sonia. She slipped me a piece of bread and butter. But why me, precisely? For the same cursed reason that "he" got me the black blouse and the turban: out of treachery, to get me into a filthy mess and have some fun at my expense.

The others were standing at the rear of the depot with their backs to us when Sonia, operating on the principle that eyes are normally located below the forehead, slipped the bread into my hand. But Sonia doesn't know the Huns or Suri Falk, who are exceptions to the rule—they have eyes in their backs, even in their heels. To say nothing of the cousins, who also see more than is proper for young girls from the "upper crust."

They saw, I knew it. They knew that I knew. They waited, turned shamelessly toward me, looking excitedly from the bread to my face and from my face to the bread. Even under the blond fringe, hunger took on a desperate and pitiful expression.

Wounded pride? Spite? The long and the short of it is that the Evil One waged a violent struggle against a reasonable person who asked nothing more than to look out for her own skin. And she seemed to have the upper hand. I knew what I had to do, it was simple. I just had to give the bread and butter to Rozzi from Dunaszerdahely, a cheerless and exhausted person who suffers from a mysterious female malady and who is watched over by her comrades with a rather unique affection: "Don't touch that, bitch!" or "Will you put down that box, dammit!" etc.

A peaceful existence, filled with esteem and friendly faces! I just had to hold out my hand . . . If only the miserable creature hadn't started picking her nose with voluptuous abandon! It wasn't disgust, but rather a desire to slap her hand, and a memory that reawakened: One day when I caught Sophie scratching her pimples, I gave her a slap on the hand. Sophie. Isn't she the one I owe this bread and butter to, if I "owe" it to anyone?

What right do they have to look at me that way? They'll just have to wait! I won't seek approval from a gang of savages! I'm not that desperate! I folded my slice of bread in half and looked in turn at the four frowning barbarians, at the "fringe" and her cousin, and at Suri, who in her excitement almost dropped her pointed chin. I turned around and calmly headed for my "office." The silence that I left behind followed me, alas, like a premonition of misfortune, like an evil spell that I had cast on myself.

Excommunicated. That's another word to which I have a "right," heavier than all the others. This is the first time that I've thought of the hill as not being the worst thing that's happened to me.

I didn't dare cry. I wouldn't give them the pleasure!

Little Suri prowled around me (which stung even more than the loneliness). Once she slipped all the way into my "office"—her little insect eyes glittering—and whispered, "The two of us, we'll be with the Poles, okay?"

"Get out!"

That was all I had the strength to say.

There I was, lower than dirt. In my misery I devoured the bread and butter all by myself, and I couldn't even taste it. No appetite anymore, that's what I've come to!

If only things had stopped there!

In front of the barracks, Sophie and the sculptress were waiting for me with mysterious looks and a well-thought-out plan. If I swiped two or three pieces of underwear a day (they felt sure that I had plenty of room under my blouse), in a few weeks we could outfit part of the barracks, the most ragged.

I looked from one to the other.

"A few weeks? That long?"

"Why? Do you have a better idea?" asked Sophie, uneasy and dirtier than ever.

"Sure, I've always found burglary more attractive than shoplifting."

They didn't say anything. Then the sculptress re-marked in a conciliatory voice that perhaps I was too tired right then, but once I was rested she hoped that I'd be kind enough to give her a few moments.

Don't be silly, of course I'm always at her disposal. But on this question it would be better to approach Suri Falk! I gave her a nice smile.

She refused to believe that I was being serious. Her reproving tone, her infuriating "morality." As if she were carrying humanity on her shoulders—all the lost souls of the earth. But she can't depend on my shoulders. That's the long and the short of it. The only lost soul I can carry is myself, and that's already more than I can handle.

"Listen to me, Madame," I said in my calmest voice.

"I'm not married," she corrected me softly.

"I don't care what you are, if you're the Pope himself. I don't meddle in your affairs. When I need guidance I'll let you know."

"You're really in a bad way," the unflappable spinster replied compassionately. "The hill didn't put you in such a state."

She wasn't wrong about that!

They didn't understand why I started laughing. It was just that I could already see the looks on their faces.

"I'm going back to the hill tomorrow. I'll recommend you as my replacement. You can just take care of the barracks, and the world, at your own risk."

With that I left them and, back in my bunk, I pretended to sleep. They didn't insist anymore.

———

Konhauser distributed thick slices of bread, topped with generous helpings of soft white cheese. I kept one half (the smaller) for Sophie; I also nibbled on her share of the cheese.

My conscience isn't clear.

Today as I slipped between the shelves I had the feeling that I was being followed, or rather "spied on." I often have the feeling that the Dunaszerdahelians and Alice don't take their eyes off me. And I? Don't I hold my breath whenever Suri or one of the barbarians gets close to the counters with the "merchandise" that we've washed, ironed, and put away? What I wouldn't give to be able to count just one of the piles of undershirts or underpants! I haven't touched anything yet. It's now out of the question to make off with anything under my blouse in order to "dress the barracks." But it's peculiar—since the sculptress's "humanitarian" dreams seem to have dimmed, the idea is beginning to tempt me; at least it no longer seems unimaginable.

—

Crime drama at the depot. Everyone bustles around, agitated and accusatory. Who would have believed it: an examining magistrate slumbered behind Alice's fringe! Sonia and Dunaszerdahely are the forces of order. The accused, judges, witnesses, even the defense is represented; a whole tribunal. There's only me as a "spectator," and Vania, the ethereal creature who continues to pace imperturbably through the depot.

The story begins with a pocket: Forty zlotys disappear from it. Sonia, the victim, completely forgets the "futility of everything" and stamps her feet, beside herself. "Pile of shit." "Gang." She swears as she dances with rage that she'd rather scrub the floor all by herself than be surrounded by "hoodlums." "Now I've seen everything," murmurs one of the Huns, because this is too much for the dignity of the famous village. The "noble" Alice is white as a sheet. "Search us," she proposes. But that's as far as things go. Someone notices that the little Falk is missing. They find her on the heap of garbage piled not far from the depot. She's cowering among the scattered bones, peelings, and other trash. She's holding the bills in her hand, and before anyone has grabbed or scolded her, she begins to swear desperately. Sonia slaps her. She's taken into custody by the Huns, still telling a touching story about a Polish uncle whom she has just run into by the greatest chance.

"Here, beside the garbage pile?" asks Alice.

To judge from her expression, she doesn't have any faith in uncles who turn up unexpectedly.

Dunaszerdahely continues more sharply.

"Big family kisses, eh?"

"Oww, oww," screams Suri, who continues to squeeze the zlotys in her paws with impressive determination (a Falk is a Falk, even under torture).

Here's the procession: Sonia in front, pink and "sizzling" like a turkey just out of the oven, followed by Dunaszerdahely with the screaming trophy, then the cousins trying to get the zlotys away from her, and finally me, who wants nothing more than to shout "Encore!" like at the opera after a bravura passage.

Watch out, we're coming to the turning point. It's waiting for us in front of the depot door. It's a small man, stocky and swarthy, with a funny face that might have been drawn by a child's hand with a thick pencil. Warszawski (the owner of this comical face) is the camp photographer; his darkroom is across from the depot. According to Frau Ellis and Sonia, "He's not a bit intellectual." Which doesn't stop him from taking excellent photos of the Germans, their girlfriends, their dogs, and sometimes even Sonia. He's a jovial fellow, close to forty; he lost a daughter my age, and he gets angry to the point of tears if anyone dares to doubt his "fundamental sadness." He's a great talker, who even manages, from time to time, to get a wan smile from Vania.

Imagine, this "fundamentally sad" man is fond of Suri. That monster! Perhaps because she's so atrociously ugly, small, and repulsive. And how would a frustrated father find clean, beautiful, lovable children at Plaszow?

"What do you want from this child?" he asks menacingly, blocking the procession.

"Owww!" screams the "child" at the top of her lungs (she wouldn't be a Falk if she didn't turn the situation to her advantage).

And the gendarmes are forced to release her.

Sonia, whom he stops from going into the depot, is hopping mad, beside herself. Frau Ellis starts yelling from inside, and Vania, the nymph, also appears in a nonspeaking role.

They would have come to blows if Sonia weren't so short and flabby. She pounds energetically on the photographer's muscular arm. He just laughs and grabs her fists, before addressing himself to her (in fact to all of us): "You'll get the zlotys back, but not till you tell us where they came from."

And since the response is a new torrent of insults, he answers for her: "You stole them."

He looks at her calmly, almost good-naturedly, lets the explosion pass, and continues: "And what's more, you stole them from our people, the ones out there dying in the dog-day heat. You steal, I steal, everyone steals—one more day, one more hour wrested from death. I'm not throwing stones, but what do you want from this kid? Come on, Suri!"

With his big paw he hugs the trembling little thing to him; she seems to hesitate between crying and smiling, and finally decides to let a smile peep through the tears.

"I'll take you into my studio," says the photographer. "I don't guarantee that you'll learn the trade, but to steal, certainly. Going through people's pockets! How dumb! Rather than swiping some things from the shelves! You'd get twice as much as the goyim who work in town, and nobody would call you a thief."

I don't dare bat an eye, but the look that passes between the cousins does not escape me. The ancestral honesty of Dunaszerdahely seems to waver.

Sonia continues to scream in Polish, German, and Yiddish (three languages that are continually mixed in this building); the wandering Vania doesn't even pretend to listen; and suddenly it occurs to me that she, too, lives by theft, by what she filches from the half-naked skeletons on the hill.

—

A slight blunder: Today I went into the darkroom unannounced. The photographer was in the process of cooking a meal for himself and Suri. They both seemed worked up, because of embarrassment or the mouth-watering vapors. I got out of there in a hurry. But Warszawski caught me and gave me a whole loaf of bread, to share among the seven of us.

Another piece of news: We'll go to roll call with the Poles, as "storekeepers." From a distance I spotted Elli Reich. Several times I tried to catch her eye, without success. (Maybe she's nearsighted.)

At roll call the Bergkapos stand on the other side of the square, Jurek more asleep than ever, handsome as a serpent.

—

The Lagerkapo has chosen the three of us, Alice, Magda, and me, to do the cleaning at the depot next door. That's where the Christian detainees leave their civilian effects, which they'll get back when they're released. We wander among the racks of dresses and suits, breathing the sweet dust of yesteryear.

"You remember my blue shantung dress, it was cut the same way," Magda says to her cousin. We stand for a long time contemplating the shantung dress like Magda's, and we sigh in unison. According to the Lagerkapo, this depot is the responsibility of the whole group; the fact that he's entrusting its maintenance to us three is not because he lacks respect for our colleagues, but because they have a hard time expressing their intelligence in German. "Intelligence," he says with a sigh, "is what I look for above all in a woman! Why is it that I only find it in pretty women?"

And there he has given us something that we thought was in suspension, in hibernation, and it was better that way. Pretty women in a camp—isn't that like flowers on a grave?

"I would never have hoped to have a writer under my authority. By the way, how is your novel coming?"

"It's not a novel, it's a journal."

"Your journal, then! What a shame I don't understand your remarkable language, which never ceases to amaze me."

"It will be translated."

"Into German?"

"Into all languages."

"Yes . . . of course . . ."

They're probably wondering whether I'm joking or

whether I'm not quite right in the head, and they put on noncommittal expressions. I don't have a smile that makes things easy.

Then the Lagerkapo moves on to Suri's story; he asks us for details, the report from A to Z. And yet his questions give the impression that he's duly informed.

"He said that to Sonia, in those words, in front of the whole group? Ha, ha, ha, ha!"

"What do you think?" I ask casually. "Were these things destined for our transport?"

"Destined." (He says it in a funny tone, with a funny smile.) "You have a poetic view of things."

I know the word is out of place, like any word at the scene of a slaughter. I know quite a few things from the photographer, including the fact that the clothes taken from us at the Auschwitz railroad station, which were supposed to be distributed among the detainees at the various camps, are part of a huge traffic of which the detainees see only the scraps. And how can you expect a commandant as "colossal" as ours (the obese man on the horse) to provide, on his salary, for his own appetite and that of his bulldog and his horses, to say nothing of the young women who don't accommodate a body like his out of pure idealism?

I prefer not to think about how our benefactor provides for his needs. To my surprise, he's the one who brings up this delicate subject. He says that he had thought of distributing everything that's left at the depot, but little is left! Barely one pair of underpants for every ten people. He's afraid it would cause a riot.

I remark that it would mean a few less cases of diarrhea. He shrugs; I just need to talk to the ladies at the depot. He doesn't have the courage, he admits; this underwear business is too much for him. We get up, it's time to start cleaning. He'd like to think that we're not going to kill ourselves at the job. Would it bother us if he took a nap? He warns us that he spends his free time sleeping, and since he has quite a bit of free time, he sleeps all day long. It's a gift from heaven, his own antidote to the war and all the insanity. He's going to tell us his dreams, he has splendid ones. With that he stretches out on the divan that we just got up from, and covers his face with a cushion that has no cover.

"One more thing," he says from under the cushion. "If anyone knocks, the first thing you have to do is wake me up. Don't open the door till afterward."

—

"You just need to talk to the ladies at the depot." I have no illusions about those ladies, but this underwear thing is beginning to bother me. I try to approach Sonia. She seems understanding, she nods, and I tell myself that we're not off to a bad start, when apropos of God knows what, on what pretext, she slips off the subject. Now all she wants to talk about is her uncle, a dentist, who gave up the ghost on the day war was declared. How lucky for him. "Just wait, I'll get you!" But she dashes toward the door, radiant, her smile both humble and dazzling.

Distinguished visitors. A young officer, and on his arm Liese—yes, it's her in the flesh, Jurek's supervisor. A carton mysteriously appears from under the counter, and a pastel raincoat emerges; Sonia, standing on tiptoe, helps her try it on. Liese still has her cheerful look (or is barely containing a hysterical laugh); she has fun showing off, bowing left and right, now gracious, now majestic. She makes everybody laugh, starting with her friend (or fiancé) and including Warszawski, the *fundamentally sad* man. Even on my face there appears—I feel it not without chagrin— a smile suitable to the occasion.

It's Warszawski's turn to dazzle us with his photos. In all of them Liese is perfect: in civilian clothes and in uniform, with and without the officer, and with a cute white cat in her arms (two little traitors). If I had a camera lens in my eye, I, too, could show her some snapshots.

In the mornings our departure rarely goes by without incident. We have to leave the barracks at dawn when the others, the "damned," go to the hill. But they don't open the depot until eight o'clock (unless there's a chance of an inspection). Add to that the storekeeper Kapo's gift for sleeping! We sometimes end up waiting for two hours in front of the "bazaar," exposed to all sorts of harassment and irritations. Scourge number one is of course the dwarf. That's the time of day when she takes her walk on the Lager-strasse, around the kitchens and washrooms. She knows perfectly well what's going on with us, but she can't stand Konhauser and every morning she pretends to be surprised.

"What are they doing here, these 'darlings'?"

She never fails to "tease" us—a matter of not losing her touch—with her riding crop.

But this morning (it must be menopause, or so they claim at the depot) she had a new idea. "Take off your clothes," she ordered—right in the middle of the Appelplatz, in front of the guard and the men sweeping up, who roared with laughter—the idea being to see if we were hiding stolen underwear beneath our blouses.

Konhauser showed up just as she was getting ready to discipline Rozzi, the Hun, who refused to get undressed (she's expecting a baby). You should have seen the looks on the "barbarians'" faces. (I don't want to think what would have happened if our chief had stayed stretched out on his couch just one more minute.)

"Put your clothes back on!" he shouted.

With our rags in our hands, we glanced at the monstrosity, who seemed to be as amused by our indecision as she was by the fury of Konhauser, who had to repeat his order.

Without a word she slashed the air with her riding crop and left, or rather faded like a specter in a horror movie. Our savior was so exhausted by the incident that he immediately withdrew for a little sleep therapy. We didn't see him again until the evening roll call. But the women were beside themselves. "Die Hexe,"[1] murmured the apathetic Vania, almost humanized with hate when she saw us with our heads bare and ghastly pale like disinterred corpses.

We learned, on that occasion, a few details about the dwarf's rise to power. In the ghetto, she betrayed the escape plan of a group that she was part of (a plan that she had cooked up herself, for that matter). Sonia was part of it, along with Frau Ellis and her two children, Konhauser and his fiancée, and a number of others. Some were finished off on the spot, and others perished in the railroad cars (Frau Ellis's two children and Konhauser's fiancée).

After four years he managed to set up this depot, of

[1] The witch.

which he became the Kapo. It was because of him
that they escaped the "actions" as "useful Jews."
"We owe everything to his energy." It seems that this
great sleeper was a fighter in his time, and that we
who have known him for a short while see only what
remains. "Remains" . . . that's all you see at Plaszow, and we have to pray that even that endures.

I observe that the war won't last forever. That
makes them laugh bitterly; their fate has nothing to
do with the war. They know too much!

If anyone will get out of it, Madame Potrez (the
dwarf) will. With what she has amassed here inside
the barbed wire, she can buy herself anything—the
Russians, the Americans, the Good Lord—the way
she bought the commandant, which wasn't really
much of a trick, because that tub of lard is as stupid as
he is evil.

"She'll succeed; everything succeeds for her."

It's a heartfelt cry from Sonia; she starts pacing the
depot in a rage. But as is her habit, she interrupts
herself in full stride, sits down, and declares, "Excuse
me, I no longer have the patience to suffer."

—

The depot is a rendezvous for the other Poles who are
also among the "remains." It serves as bistro, post
office, and casino; there they exchange news, gossip,

nightmares. All at once I'm there alone with Vania. I dutifully take advantage of the opportunity, and start wandering with her from one corner of the depot to the other. I briefly explain to her the idea that I haven't been able to convince Sonia of. I can't tell what she thinks of it, I can't see her face because she's always a step in front of me.

"But how many of you are there, in the barracks?"

"Two thousand."

I'm suddenly out of my depth; it's ludicrous. Nevertheless I conscientiously begin again: Every life matters, and the cystitis, and the diarrhea, etc. But with a gesture she dismisses my "tirade" like a bothersome noise.

For a second she looks at me the way I must have looked at the sculptress when she made her incongruous proposal. Then she shrugs her shoulders. She's letting it drop! No, she's just continuing her stroll.

"So why don't you hand them out?"

"What?" (Is she making fun of me?)

"It's very simple," she says as she strolls. "You get them together here, and you hand the things out."

"But . . ." (I'm stammering. She understands.)

"If you like, I'll come help you after closing."

Suddenly I don't feel well.

"When?" I ask, raising my voice (it's impossible for me to keep up at such a moment).

"Whenever you like. Today, for example."

"Really? You're not kidding?"

"Please leave me alone now," she says, worn out from talking so much.

We finally come to an agreement: It'll be tomorrow. In the meantime I'll alert the sculptress, so she can choose among the most ragged. What if we rounded up the whole barracks and . . . God, I hope she's not joking with me, this creature of dreams.

—

I still haven't introduced Fredy. How is that possible? The real, genuine Fredy is back at school with the stuffed owls, squirrels, and ducks. One time, before anatomy class, we dressed him from head to foot: overcoat, galoshes, and the prof's hat. A mischievous boy hid behind him, and when the prof came in, the skeleton saluted him with his own hat. Result: We were kept after class to write two hundred times "I will not mock the human body."

Who would have thought that I'd see that "body" again before the end of vacation—although in separate pieces—and that I'd "mock" those pieces to the extent of walking on them?

Our "meeting" today was unexpected, nevertheless. First, I wasn't walking, but lying in the sand be-

hind the depot—lacking the nerve to go in and not
knowing where to go or what to do with my undesir-
able self. They haven't yet dismissed me, but the air
is unbreathable. Sonia's breaking her neck to per-
suade the Lagerkapo to fire me. It's no longer worth
the trouble to take care of my lamé blouse. I'm
stretched out, waiting for dark, waiting for the hours
to pass and take away my nausea. To take me away.
And suddenly I feel myself being bumped, or rather
"poked," by a finger in my back. Getting up, I see in
the sand one of Fredy's hands, a complete hand with
all its bones perfectly preserved. It has just beckoned
to me! In other times I might have screamed, but in
my situation you can't reject any advance, however
"bony" it may be.

"Come on, Fredy, give me your paw! You're so
peaceful and cool. And you don't shove, you don't hit,
you don't throw stones!" (As a gesture of gratitude,
I'll bury it one day.)

Living hands! Hundreds and hundreds, held out
toward me menacingly. "Here, here, here! Give me
that shirt, come on!" I'm not Christ; how can I put
eighty shirts into five hundred hands?

Vania the nymph handed me the piles of underwear
one after the other, impassive as a well-tuned, well-
oiled machine. After the last assault, when we found
ourselves empty-handed in front of the empty

shelves, and the rocks started flying, I ducked back inside the depot. I called to Vania, but she remained on the threshold, motionless. At one point I thought I heard her laugh, and I said to myself that it was hysteria. But the hysterics came later. Sonia and Frau Ellis arrived in a state that's easy to imagine. No one beat me; Vania took responsibility for it all with the sort of serene patience that made Sonia scream that she's raving mad, everybody knows it, and they'll all end up at Auschwitz. Crazy? That's not what I think! I suspect she's royally amused, and that in fact she's just a nymph who's a little twisted and who unwinds when she can.

It was dark, fortunately, when I got back to the barracks. Sophie and the sculptress, my accomplices, were asleep or pretending to be. And all at once something happened that was much more harrowing than the punches, the insults, and Sonia put together.

On my hand I felt a soft, wet, hot mouth: "Thank you, dear, thank you." I jumped as if she had bitten me. It was "Madame." Great God! She who could be my mother, and who once handed out such big tips!

Oh, Fredy, was it this lousy for you, too, when you were still on this side?

—

Everything's quiet in the barracks, in the depot, in the camp. Sonia's resentment seems to have calmed or chilled; she comes and goes in front of the empty shelves and doesn't breathe a word.

It happened at roll call. The count was off. They had counted us a dozen times. Did we wait for minutes, for hours? (Maybe when you're terrified there are only centuries.) The dwarf danced around on her high heels; all alone in the middle of the huge square she strutted constantly like an exasperated little idiot.

One was missing.

She was found in one of the barracks, asleep on her mattress.

With her hands crossed behind her back, the dwarf started walking around the poor girl—who, dazed and not quite awake, in turn circled around the dwarf. Finally the Pole stopped and motioned to Otto, one of the Lagerkapos. At that moment the silence became complete, as if thousands of people had stopped breathing at the same time, and I knew that the girl was lost. But she didn't know. She looked at the monstrosity with a sort of trust, as if to say: But I didn't do anything, I was just sleeping.

I had seen Otto at roll call. He's a German, and as a *Schwerverbrecher* he was condemned to eleven years in prison, before the war; a Goliath with brush-cut hair, fat, with a red face covered with freckles (even his big, thick hand is sprinkled with them). He gestured to the girl, who approached, and ordered her to hold out her hands. Docilely, like at school, she obeyed.

The riding crop struck twice; she groaned but stayed on her feet.

"Take off your clothes!"

Her bloody hands tried to unbutton the white blouse, but didn't have the strength. Otto ripped it off with his hand. He took off his leather jacket and put it on the ground after folding it carefully. This calm, careful way of preparing for her murder upset me more than everything that followed.

Fortunately, she fainted almost at once. Otto continued to strike until he was out of breath. He was drenched in sweat, his shirt sticking to his skin; what he was hitting was now only a thing. His job was done, and he kept at it purely for pleasure. He loves this. The dwarf finally stopped him. Bending over the corpse, she raised its head with her high heel. Otto wiped his forehead. They carried her away, she who had ceased to be a number. The roll call continued.

—

I'm alive! I'm writing . . . I'm "enjoying myself," not like Otto, but I'm choosing my words, "composing." I'm plying a traitor's trade, and the deeper I go and the better I get at betrayal, the more right I have to the name "writer." It doesn't matter that it's myself I'm betraying first and foremost! At this very moment I'm about to unburden myself of a painful secret; it's like a wound that once the scab is off runs the risk of becoming infected. I half beg myself to be quiet, for my peace of mind and for Sophie's. In fact it's already too late . . . Sophie, for her part, keeps silent; could she be afraid, too? "Friendship," "my friend"; words that people use loosely, when they should put them aside and protect them, and say them only rarely and solemnly!

When did the breach open? If I had known, I would have tried something. The hideous, senseless breakdowns. When we pull ourselves together the breach is no longer a breach but a gulf. We stand helpless on the edge. We don't know how to build a bridge across the void. Do we really want to?

Maybe it started with the depot. Sophie encouraged me: "What good would it do for both of us to kill ourselves in the sun or get soaked? We'll still have time to ourselves." But in the evening, when I come back from the depot with my head buzzing with stories, she struggles to stay awake as she listens to them because they aren't *our* stories, and her own story is one of exhaustion and hunger, period. Which reminds me of the piece of bread and butter that I devoured in secret. When does the silence between two people begin to "smell" sneaky? At what point do you start to dodge your conscience, to avoid it like a trap?

Of course, I make an effort (as often as possible) to

place my offerings on the altar of friendship. "I make an effort"—that doesn't sound much like friendship. And it isn't really with the best of feelings that I set aside for her half of any bread or cheese that someone slips me at the depot. No one has any idea how mouth-watering such a set-aside half can be! I look at it, engrossed, sometimes I nibble it a little and then close the bag again with a heavy heart. Resentment? Embarrassment? Or both? Sometimes, if my horrible appetite overwhelms what remains of my conscience, and sinking into contemptibility I devour everything that I had saved for her, the remorse weighs on me more than the hunger did. So it isn't worth it. So why? Who's to blame for all this trouble? Is it surprising that I'm sometimes irritated with her, curt and uncommunicative? But whatever my mood she doesn't react, too exhausted or discreet. Which irritates me even more. Finally I pull myself together and abruptly become talkative and affectionate, which leaves her just as inert as my other excesses. As knowing and "old" as she is, she must have seen through me ages ago. Our relations are more and more reserved, tense, almost false, including our silences.

I tear myself away from my notes less and less often. Where is the philosophizing, our long chats of before? "It would be so sad if we ended up not talking about anything but our bread ration!" she said to me one day. I'm nostalgic for that day, for the old Sophie. I'd like to get her back. But what's stopping me, really? Oh, trivial things! The way she turns away when I hand her the package, ashamed of her hunger. She eats it in secret. But one time when she thought I was asleep I watched her from under my eyelids: She started out nibbling, then threw herself on the bread, greedily. Then she withdrew it carefully from her mouth, and before she took another bite she looked for a long time at the marks of her teeth on the bread.

Pity! A torment that I was spared when we were dragging our shovels on the hill! And the smells! Her filthy neck, I never noticed it before! But how can I hold that against her, when I take a shower every day?

Noises didn't aggravate me before, either. My sleep has become light, my nerves on edge. I have a hard time understanding: Why burst into the barracks yelling, stomping on one another's toes like savages, when everyone ends up getting a ration of bread? Sophie comes in with that same wild look. "Is it here, the bread?" Two weeks ago I didn't even notice it, I rushed to my bunk with the same expression of an Indian on the warpath.

—

A carload of Dutch sabots has arrived. Not surprising that the commandant didn't find any buyers in the entire Reich; they're as heavy as toboggans to drag around. A little underwear is mixed in; it must be what came to hand during a quick raid, or was so dirty it was "deported" to us. The perspiration of an entire convoy came with it. The smell of transport! I would recognize it anywhere: the smell of thirsty, crowded, unclean bodies. Sonia was nauseated. It was all moved to the disinfection hut. We were disappointed to find that it consisted mostly of men's underpants. Which didn't stop us from appropriating them (with the prior permission of Konhauser), four pairs each, better than nothing. Ironing them, putting them away, talk about a chore! It didn't go without a fuss, because of the pregnant Hun who insisted on doing the ironing, and stood up to the other Huns, who were hollering and swearing out of "affection" as usual. Where does she get this rage to work when she can barely stand up?

I can't help watching her. I'm not the only one. Her insignificant self is at the center of a violent struggle between the tribe and the Poles at the depot. The Huns defend their position with gestures reinforced by the only word they know in the language of Goethe and Adolf: *Nein.* Our bosses (including the photographer) constantly shower the mother-to-be with "disgraceful" advice; they even take it upon themselves to bring a specialist to the depot, an "angel-maker" who has been practicing her *specialty* at the camp for years.

"You can keep your angel-maker," grumble the Huns.

"Here they kill babies, they strangle them or give them a shot . . . Don't you understand?"

"I don't care what you say. We'll never believe that the Good Lord would allow that."

I translate, and only then do the Poles start loudly unburdening themselves of everything that the Good Lord allows to happen on earth, and at Plaszow in particular . . .

"But tiny babies!"

The Huns are immovable.

"No, nobody touches our Rozzi! This little one, she's been looking forward to it so much!"

"What do you think will happen to it here?"

"Whatever happens to the rest of us."

The mother listens to all this uproar, not looking very concerned. But once she nudges me with her elbow: "If they do what you say to children, what becomes of the mother?"

"She becomes an angel, too, I suppose."

"Together?"

"Yes."

We hoped that would make her think, and in fact she must have thought about it, because after a moment she said to me, "It's better that way."

In the afternoon the cousins tried, but with no greater success.

"The Good Lord wouldn't allow it."

"But what if, nevertheless . . . ?"

"Then He doesn't exist," she said, "so why live?"

They feed her all day long, and yet she continues to grow thinner. Even her poor belly seems to be shrinking. Perhaps the baby for whom she's ready to die is already dead.

—

The news that "merchandise" had arrived preceded us to the barracks. Anyone who has never seen a miracle had something to open their eyes this evening: Our neighbors have learned to greet us. At the door an odd quartet, ragged and determined, attached itself to me; "Madame," my insufferable neighbor, was among them. I was showered with compliments; it was like being carried across the barracks on a dish of honey. I was compared to a plane tree, a cedar, Deanna Durbin, Joan of Arc; I felt like I was drowning in sweetness and I rushed to my bunk, disgusted, and disappeared under my blanket but still wasn't able to calm down. I'm seething. The indignity of these old women exasperates me.

I can hear "Madame" crying; she's crying to be heard, of course. Which doesn't mean that she isn't crying for good reason.

"My husband was the director of a clinic," she wails. "I was the most spoiled woman in N. Do you think it's easy for me to lower myself? You can see how hard it is for me! I would never do it for myself. But the little one is anemic, we've always worried about her lungs. When I hear her coughing in her sleep, I tell myself there's nothing so shameful that I wouldn't do it for a ration of marmalade or butter."

"Calm down," I say, and I slip two pairs of underpants into her hand.

I didn't know Sophie was watching me. How long? For the first time I see her angry; she cries, she yells, she calls me inconsiderate.

"Come on, come on," I say, "it's nothing, I'll bring you some others . . ."

She calms down at once but remains on her guard.

"Really? How many?"

"Two." (I'm also on my guard.) "But what will you do with them?"

"Don't worry about that," she says, with such a determined look that I'm intrigued. "All you have to do is bring them! And stop looking at me like that! There's nothing wrong with me! It's just that I've decided to steal and kill. I want to eat till I'm full one time, just one time, even if they hang me!"

—

Sophie and I go up to the "nice neighborhood." That's what we shorn heads call the neat little "town" where, in painted barracks decorated with velvety fabrics of every color, the natives have their nests.

The "nests" were still crowded a year ago, and their cleanliness left something to be desired. But they became more spacious and comfortable after each "action." Piles of blankets and pillows, a whole trousseau, waited on the bunks for those who escaped. Not long ago, you made your will before every roll call. To avoid misunderstandings, each person wrote on a scrap of paper the name of the person to whom she left her pillow, her blanket, and her summer and winter things, just in case . . .

"We never knew," Frau Ellis says, "who would come back from roll call. Those who were 'selected' for the 'action' had to first dig their graves, then after stripping and placing everything they were wearing on the ground—(in proper order: clothes on one side, underwear on the other)—they had to kneel at the edge of the ditch and wait for the bullets in the back. Bullets that the Germans made the Jewish 'leaders' of the camp pay for. Economizing on ammunition meant that the work was often botched, and cries rose from the ditches for hours after the execution. During large 'actions' things moved too fast. There was no question of burying the bodies, they were simply covered with sand, so you could no longer tell whether you were walking on bones that were old or recent. Everything happened so fast that you didn't even have time to see your mother or sister vanish. We were no longer capable of suffering, or of being scared or surprised. Death is only frightening to the living. We hadn't been that for a long time."

And yet . . . they all conscientiously distributed their pillows, their blankets, and their spoons, to avoid "misunderstandings." Such meticulousness in the face of a death that is no longer a "drama" but an everyday incident, plain and unadorned! And here are these dolls draped in inherited bathrobes, among their inherited blankets and pillows, having their tea parties, powdering their noses, defying at every moment their unbelievable memories; after all, it's only by the barest chance that others don't languish in their place, in the same bathrobes, under the same blankets, spreading their bread with white cheese and meticulously drawing the outlines of their lips.

"And I," says Sophie, who hasn't the least desire to let herself be moved by any of that, "will sell these underpants to someone!"

To my pained surprise she starts offering the "merchandise" in her German, which is as bad as Ruchi Falk's: "Wäsche, reine Wäsche, bilige, reine Wäsche!"[1]

She catches me unprepared. Isn't that Sonia laugh-

[1] Underwear, clean underwear, cheap, clean underwear!

ing, over there in the window? No, it's my breathing . . .

"Are you nuts?" I whisper, pinching her arm. "Don't act like an idiot. Who would need these rags?"

She doesn't even answer me. As if possessed by an alien will, she drags me along and tortures me with her Falk voice: "Wäsche, reine, bilige Wäsche, bitte."

On the bunks no one moves. What appalls me seems to be part of the routine here. Yet finally a beautiful and distracted white hand reaches out: "Let me see."

Sophie turns pale and hands her a pair of underpants. She rejects them. I feel better. Sophie digs in her heels and looks at the young Polish woman humbly but inflexibly. Finally the woman has had enough, and offers a ridiculously low price to get rid of her.

I stand to one side, as a way of showing that I have nothing to do with it. Sophie lets out a torrent of excited words. I'm again overcome with rage, and I'm ready to intervene when I realize, dumbfounded, that the Polish woman is answering her. Yes, it looks to me like a dialogue. They're bargaining. My anger subsides.

"A quarter," says the Polish woman.

"A half," responds Sophie.

I want to break in: "Don't insist, you idiot!" But Sophie gestures to me to shut up. According to her, impatience is the enemy of any transaction; she continues the discussion with the same flabbergasting tenacity.

When we finally return, with half a loaf of bread covered with a thick layer of white cheese, she's too worn out to celebrate.

"It's funny," I remark. "Surely she didn't need a pair of men's underpants!"

"That's the trick," Sophie the "expert" informs me. "To get rid of a piece of merchandise that nobody needs, at a price that you yourself think is scandalous."

I observe that it's begging, but never mind!

"The bread's fresh," she answers, "but we shouldn't nibble it like that."

I haven't touched it, she's the one who's constantly picking at it with her dirty fingers. Is she doing it unconsciously, while she soliloquizes?

"Listen: If in the first few minutes they agree to half a slice more, that means that after half an hour the deal will be wrapped up."

At last she notices the "ravages" that she's inflicted on our bread, and apologizes.

"It doesn't matter," I say. "Tell me, where did you get this business experience?"

She shrugs.

"Where? From life . . ."

Life! She talks about it only rarely. In fact I didn't know much about what her life was like when we weren't in class. But I do remember that she gave private lessons. She didn't accept anything from her parents, and was proud of it. She rented a bed. Her landlady unscrewed the lightbulb in the evening when she went to sleep (which was never later than eight o'clock). Sophie worked by the light of an oil lamp, and at school she reeked so strongly of oil that sitting beside her I smelled, too.

"What do you expect me to do?" she said, annoyed. "It gets into my clothes."

One day I went to get her at the home of one of her students, and in the entry I heard the chambermaid lecturing her: "You're going to ruin the floor again with those cursed boots! You need to wear galoshes when you visit nice homes, little one!"

"How could you let that old bag talk to you like that?" I asked, indignant.

She shrugged.

"You don't understand, you've never worked in nice homes . . ."

P.S.: An unexpected meeting that I almost forgot. Coming back we noticed our two distinguished co-workers, Alice and Magda, in the middle of a group; they were selling underpants. I almost said hello to them, but Sophie stopped me.

"Come on," she said, "they wouldn't be happy to see us."

I can believe it!

———

"They" are coming! That's how Ruchi Falk greeted us; better not to get undressed, "they" might show up any time after midnight, and we wouldn't have time to put on our clothes.

We're indifferent to these "prophecies." Everyone gets ready for the night.

In the daytime I know it: They're close. But at night my optimism abandons me, and I buckle. The night is German, and what am I against the night? And why should I be the one who comes through it? We don't even have the hope that a condemned man has: an appeal for mercy. We're not guilty of anything, we're simply "undesirables." Bullets are a waste; if it were possible, they'd exterminate us like flies, with Flytox. I have a desperate desire for a sharp physical pain, a pain that would cancel out all the rest, that would make me scream. I let out a groan to see what happens. Sophie doesn't move, nor does the sculptress. Yet it's impossible for them not to have heard me, the fair-weather friends. They know everything that I know, and still they're snoozing or pretending to.

I ask out loud, abruptly, "Are you asleep?"

Sophie doesn't stir, but a muffled grunt answers from my left: "What's wrong?"

"Nothing." I sit up. "Are they going to leave us to the Russians? What do you think?"

"Of course."

"No, we know too much."

Where do I get the uncontrollable desire to give her my nightmares? But I've made a poor choice of victim. She defends her rest.

"Try to sleep," she says darkly.

"With these thoughts?"

"Don't think about it!"

"Stop kidding yourself, it may be only a matter of hours. We're as good as dead."

Furious, she pulls the blanket over her head.

"Are you really going to sleep? How on earth can you?"

"The same way you can," says the voice from under the blanket, and adds, "Word of honor, if I weren't so sleepy, I'd stay awake just to shake you every half hour."

As if she didn't know that I suffer from chronic insomnia. I don't have nerves of steel and global concerns! The fate of my insignificant self torments me ceaselessly. I no longer expect any help. I flop back on the mattress, knowing that until morning I'll be prey to this waking torture.

So I'm awake. And yet someone wakes me up, at least someone or something makes me jump. At first it's the bed that seems to be pitching, then the entire building. "Bombardment" is my first thought, when I wake from my state of wakefulness.

"Owww . . . owww . . . owww . . . !"

It's very close to me: a prolonged wail, interrupted by the cries of someone in agony, a person on the point of dying, or several?

I don't dare open my eyes. And yet nothing actually visible can compare to my visions. It's the end . . . But no—shit!

It's the Falks praying, turned toward the east. Kneeling on their bed, they're continually bending forward, banging their heads against the boards. The three of them are doing it together, simultaneously, tirelessly. (Not surprising that they yell louder with each jolt; after a while these gymnastics must be hard on even a Falk's skull.)

Boom, boom, "Owww, owww." That's the rhythm of this strange choir. On the bunks everyone is up, dazed with sleep.

People protest, hollering from all directions.

"Stop it, the Good Lord isn't deaf."

"Owww . . . !" (Their yelling, as if they're possessed by a holy frenzy, is becoming intolerable.)

"Stop, dammit!"

I'd almost like to jump on them, but in spite of

everything it's a show I don't want to interrupt: Ruchi on her knees with her arms raised, making a sales pitch to the Lord—she looks like an exorcist in a trance. The wailing doesn't stop, or the "booms" either; they pretend they can't see or hear anything. But they can see and hear us perfectly well. Their "ecstasy" doesn't fool anyone, and certainly not the Lord Above, who is supremely perceptive (provided He's at His post!).

"Do you think banging your heads on the wood is enough to make Him close His eyes to your filthy schemes?"

Ruchi jumps on me. She claws me with as much energy as she was using to cozy up to God!

"Look who's talking, you little bitch, goy, whore!"

"At least I'm not banging my head against the boards."

Of what followed, I don't have a very clear memory. I only know that we did a lot of pinching and spitting in each other's faces. Then I remember only a sort of large ball in which I was rolling, together with a number of others; sometimes I was digging my knees into somebody, sometimes other people were walking on my stomach. When we separated, through force or fatigue, I was overcome by a delicious lethargy. Unfortunately, it was already morning.

At the depot we made a big impression with our

swollen faces, covered with bruises and everything . . .

"What happened?"

"Bombardment!" said Suri, giving me a friendly
wink.

———

Distribution of boots. The usual line in front of the
depot. After a real hand-to-hand, rumpled and with
my turban askew, I finally go to see Konhauser (at the
"Christian" depot). As luck would have it, he isn't
sleeping this time and hears me knock. Of course I
can stay and work, until evening if I like.

It's cool inside. The silence is a blessing. Does he
expect me to start working right away? He's watching
me, which is more intimidating than a whole barracks
in a free-for-all. I have to get used to his presence, be
detached about it! That's all I have in mind. His
question comes as a relief. A chat! I much prefer that.

He: What are you writing about, exactly?

Me: Everything and nothing.

He: For example?

Me: Whatever comes into my head. You, for example.

He: Really? And what do you say about me?

Me: That you sleep all the time.

He: Lately I suffer from insomnia. It's hard for me

to get eleven hours (sigh). What would you suggest I do? Should I keep a journal?

Me: Why not?

He: Do you think I'm intelligent?

I nod my head.

He: As a matter of fact I am, enough to know that I have nothing to add to what's already been said.

Me: What if you're just lazy?

He: Perhaps it's the fate of the mediocre.

Me: Or the excuse of a slacker. Who says that image of yourself is accurate?

He: I'll tell you a very big secret. (He leans toward me and says, very low:) Every human being has a true image of himself. Not all day long, but two minutes a day at least. During those two minutes the count is right: You know what you are and what you're worth! Those two minutes of clarity are what you fight for, why you struggle all day long.

Me: And during those two minutes, who are you?

He: A boy who's rather nice and nobody's fool, who knows how to tickle a keyboard, who has read *Zarathustra*, etc. But if forty-two years ago his poor parents had read the newspaper instead of conceiving him, that wouldn't have created a void anywhere, an empty place, Ludwig Konhauser's place.

Me: And if Ludwig van Beethoven's parents had done the same thing, do you think anyone would have felt a big void, wept and so on?

He: You really aren't stupid.

Me: No! And I think that if I disappeared I'd miss myself terribly.

We laugh.

"And yet," I add, "I've had moments when my only desire was to vanish painlessly and forever."

He asks whether that was when I was separated from my family. I say no. I was alone on a train when I was arrested; I was in the ghetto (it was actually a brickyard) with strangers. I got away several times. They caught me. I remember all that only vaguely. The one moment that I don't think I can ever forget was after my last escape, when I stopped wanting to get away, wanting anything at all, and that was a moment of great solace and peace. It was the precise moment when at the brickyard I saw the huge crowd of people and I said to myself: "Wherever they go, I'll go; whatever happens to them will happen to me." Maybe it's because of that great fatigue that I don't remember the railroad cars or anything up until the Waschraum, as if I had been on holiday from myself, anesthetized.

He's heard all that. That's everyone's story—more or less. What interests him at the moment is how I see myself during the two minutes in question.

I say that there are moments when I feel completely worn out, so ridiculous I could die.

"Why?"

"Because all the rest of the time I want to take a bite out of the world . . ."

He looks me up and down without a word, and I hasten to add that it may just be my youth, that it's an "excessive" age . . . According to him, it's not a matter of age, but of appetite. Should I be envied or pitied? He can't decide. And he adds with his usual open and mischievous smile, "But if you were a racehorse, I'd bet on you."

I don't even know what I said to him, because I was as dazzled as if he had set the sun to blazing on my face.

—

Hard to fathom the silence: secret jubilation or restrained panic? As if I were waiting somewhere in a void, and the day and the night were rushing toward me at the same speed, with no sign to let me know which of the two would arrive first.

Or it may be another compromise, something temporary and incomplete.

Okay, I'll vegetate. Breathe for one more day, one more page!

—

"Do you care a lot about your journal?"

The question chills me. (Is Konhauser afraid of a search?) I must have turned pale.

"Look, nobody wants to take your journal away from you."

One day I had said to him that I'd like to know it was out of the camp, safe. An opportunity has presented itself. Someone is leaving the camp today, someone whom he knows and who surely won't be bothered on the way out. If I give him the address of one of my Christian friends, this person will do whatever it takes to get it to them.

"Where?" I ask stupidly. "If it were lost . . ."

I'm annoying him, and he continues dryly: "There are no guarantees, this is war, there are only chances. Tomorrow we may both be strolling in Cracow."

"Then why should I give it up?"

His face darkens.

"Because there's another possibility."

I only have a few minutes to think about it. It's better that way; my indecision will be the same in one hour or ten. In the end I have only one concern, remembering the name of our concierge on Stanislo Street: Sebök or Sebes? As if everything depended on that address. As soon as it comes to me, I write it on the cover in big round letters. He has already prepared a dressing for the "wound," two small notebooks.

"You have to learn to write in small, tight letters," he suggests. "That's preferable."

I drag out the cleaning in order to see with my own

eyes the lucky mortal who a few hours from now will be strolling the streets, taking the train of his own free will, and carrying away my "testimony," as the sculptress calls it.

It can only be a German who has served his sentence. I think of a "light political" like the designer who left a few days ago. There are also the "ordinary law" prisoners, like Otto, who leaves today.

I have the honor of bringing him fresh underwear from our depot. Sonia and Frau Ellis wander among the counters for a long time before choosing a red checked shirt and a pair of briefs big enough to hold an elephant's butt. When I show up with these two charming items under my arm, Otto is in the process of trying on his old jacket.

"No," he says sadly, taking it off. "I've gotten too big. It doesn't fit me anymore, and besides, it's shabby."

"Yes," agrees Konhauser seriously, "a real tough guy has to have his self-respect."

As he hands him another jacket, he gives me an amused glance behind his back.

The golem sighs.

"You're telling me!"

He looks despondent, trying on jackets that are all too tight, and starts bemoaning his lot: He's gotten used to the camp, eating and drinking his fill, too many women to count!

"There's no shortage of them outside, either," Konhauser consoles him, "thanks to the war."

But the war doesn't thrill Otto. What will he do outside, in a world turned upside down, with a trade as precarious as his? They'll stick him in a munitions plant. Hustle, Otto, move the heavy crates! And that isn't the worst: They're emptying the prisons, so it's said, and sending them all to the front! Boom, boom! No more Otto . . . Kaput!

Funny to see this butcher going over his little miseries, self-pitying fear on his insolent and obtuse mug! And Konhauser, who seems to share his worries like a brother.

"You're lucky," sighs the gangster, "you can take it easy till the end of the war. Ein nettes Leben, ein ruhiges Leben."[1] (His little pig eyes are wet with emotion.) "Ich bin kein Antisemit; du bist mein Freund."[2]

"Ja!" agrees Konhauser. "So ist es im Leben, man muss scheiden."[3]

The giant sobs.

"Aber wir bleiben Freunde, nicht wahr?"[4]

[1] A pleasant life, a quiet life!
[2] I'm not an anti-Semite; you're my friend.
[3] Such is life, people have to part.
[4] But we'll stay friends, won't we?

He's going to kiss him, I say to myself, horrified. But he just takes him by the arm and walks him as far as the door.

Why did Konhauser take my notebook from the table? No, it's too unthinkable for me to panic. What are they plotting on the doorstep? Why are they talking so low? What if I made a grab for it? But I'd have to do it in a wheelchair, my legs are made of cotton.

"Ein naiver Kerl, dieser Otto," says my friend as he comes back in. "Der Arme fürchtet, er wäre der einzige Verbrecher im Reich."[1]

"Where's my notebook?"

"In his bag, I suppose."

My question seems to annoy him.

"He's a murderer . . . a brute . . ."

That's all I manage to say.

"Which won't keep him from reading an address. That brute saved me twice from the *Sonderkommando*. You're a writer, you ought to know: Perfection doesn't exist! With brutes any more than with saints! I know contemptible ones who would let themselves be drawn and quartered for a pal!"

"I want my notebook!"

I throw myself onto the mattress but, unable to cry, I rage dry-eyed.

---

[1] A naive guy, Otto. The poor fellow is afraid he'll be the only criminal in the Reich.

He looks at me in silence, then goes to the table, fills a glass with water, and empties it in my face.

I stand up, speechless.

It's not too late, he says. If I want him to, he'll catch Otto and bring me back my notebook. He waits, looking me up and down coldly. I don't move. I don't want anything, except to vanish, disintegrate on the spot . . .

This morning he summoned Alice and Magda alone to do the cleaning.[1]

—

Air raids one after another; the Fritzes seem nervous! Which translates into a jubilant mood in the camp. Sonia and Warszawski, the two old enemies, embraced each other today at the depot. Rozzi, who has been completely collapsed for the past several days, sometimes looks at us with the eagerness of a dog that thinks it hears its master's step on the stairs. Could the Cassandras at the depot have forgotten their "prophecies"?

Today we're riding the crest of the wave. We get two whole loaves of bread, with a mountain of white cheese. I don't touch mine. In the evening, a feast on the bunk—Sophie, me, the sculptress, and "Ma-

[1] Otto got the notebook to our concierge, and it became the core of this book.

dame" with her whiny daughter. Madame seems suddenly older, and disturbingly plainspoken. Nothing more about her Rosenthal china, her designer furniture, her husband the clinic director—not a word. On the other hand, the crybaby seems to be prospering; she has even dug up an older Polish man, a "gentleman." She has her turban, like all the bald women with any self-respect, and solemnly announces, "When this is over, I'm going to take a bath."

Sophie eats silently, engrossed. Sometimes when we speak to her she seems shocked, like a believer interrupted in the middle of her devotions.

—

Solitude. The Russians are almost here, apparently.

Faced with a great joy, we're at almost as much of a loss as if we were faced with a great misfortune.

Today Konhauser asked specifically for Alice and Magda to do his cleaning.

It's clear he doesn't want anything more to do with me.

I'm afraid I'll take this slap in the face with me to freedom.

—

A nightmare that I've been struggling with all day: I'm looking for Mama. Weeping, I walk around a shut-tered house. I knock at an iron door, tall and menacing. Mysterious women (nothing but women) go in and out. They push me aside and give me bizarre, ambiguous explanations that only increase my uneasiness. "Your mother is inside, we're taking care of her." Or "Don't worry . . . you'll see her soon." "When? What are you doing to her?" I shout, and I force my way through, I push someone aside, several people perhaps. Using my fists and elbows, I make it to the stairway; there they finally let me go, but my dread ripens into terror as I rush up the steps. The doors are wide open; I run through several rooms and find Mama in the last one. She's almost a skeleton; the skin clinging to her bones is bluish, her withered, unrecognizable face is blue, and the two glassy globes of her eyes are sunk in deep sockets. The woman holding her in her arms is the one who just now tried to stop me from going up. She holds her in such a way that her stiffened limbs and her sweet head hang down, her long hair, lusterless and dead, almost touching the floor. "They've killed her," I say to myself. But I can't accuse them, because the women are many and I have no proof.

Since then I've been obsessed by the mysterious house, looking for a way to get there and catch the criminal women, as if it weren't a dream but a warning, an ominous message.

I'll never see my mother again. I don't "feel" it; *I know it* with a sad certainty, like death, like the changing of the seasons. I no longer hope. I'm in mourning, a calm and chronic mourning. As I try to patch up my wound, I sometimes find that I'm becoming familiar with the irreparable, like a seasoned orphan.

How do I know? Bah, all this unfathomable, inscrutable stuff, all my labyrinths where I sometimes wander in spite of myself, but without bringing back a clear image or anything coherent. Maybe it's fortunate not to know the gulf over which you're passing.

I know that I'd only have to stop for a single instant and I'd be overwhelmed. I don't stop. High waves carry away the wreckage of what was my childhood. And I, washed up on the shore alone, watch it go. Sometimes it's my bedroom that emerges, my sofa bed with the white-spotted blue spread, a table leg decorated with stick figures, trees, and other doodles from the time when I still couldn't reach the drawer, and the big desk pad with the old blotter on which I practiced my signature hundreds of times: here the autograph of a star, somewhere else the small writing of a dependable worker, the writing of someone about whom her friends say, at the height of her fame, "And yet she remained so unassuming . . ." My couch with the broken springs, the hollows made by my body, the flowers on the upholstery. I spent hours there, wandering in that world of petals: There were haughty ones, and humble ones, too, beautiful, healthy petals and embittered proletarian ones, circling together endlessly or quiet and solitary, making enigmatic signs to me with their stems . . .

I'll never see that upholstery again, that room. I'll never again daydream on my dear swaybacked couch.

—

I return from the disinfection hut with a big package of underwear (the other storekeepers are still there). I find Jurek sitting on the counter, swinging his long legs, which are bare below his short pants.

We're alone. My hope is the photographer. When I left he was still busy in the darkroom. I hear Jurek's drawling, nasal voice.

"Give me a shirt, but make it something nice."

"Wait till the women come back," I say, or rather, a sort of automaton says through my lips.

"Aren't you a woman?" he asks, shooting me a sleepy look from under his eyelids.

I can't come up with an answer. I pretend not to have heard; I move toward the door without haste, so as not to let him see that I'm feeling uneasy. He doesn't jump down from the counter; he waits until I'm next to him and crosses his legs around my waist. I don't have time to get loose or scream because I have to concentrate on breathing, as if I were in danger of drowning. I have to push away this heaviness, this heat! A violent pulse (I don't know whether it's coming from my chest or the other chest pressed against mine); I shove my hand against that other chest. He lets go of me too abruptly. Did I slip? I don't remember hitting myself, because long before that everything went dark.

When I come to, I'm stretched out on the counter. Warszawski is there, talking in Yiddish with Jurek, who is still sitting on the counter. His singsong intonation is like Ruchi Falk's. I see for the first time from close up the badly shaven profile, the circles around his eyes; from below he looks like an old, sleepy Jew.

They're talking about me. Jurek says that I must be "stuck up," that the boys probably chased after me with chocolates . . . that it isn't normal to pass out when he was just kidding around.

I open my eyes and prop myself up on my elbows. I ask him what he did before, whether he was in school. I ask questions like I would with any boy. He was an apprentice optician, and he doesn't see what I find funny about that. I don't know either, I must be hysterical.

Later the photographer brings tea, and Jurek assures me that he didn't mean to do me any harm, quite the contrary. He adds that if before long we should meet "on the other shore," I shouldn't count on him. It would be too late to have any fun.

This "joke" delights both of them.

"It's hardly likely that we'll see each other again," I say.

"Why?"

I take his whip and crack it in the air.

"Because of that. They grill murderers like pigs over there."

He grimaces.

"You're nothing but a pain in the neck," he says. "I've never killed—Yes, once," he corrects himself with a gloomy look.

"Who?"

He shrugs his shoulders, takes the whip from me, touches two fingers to his forehead in a salute, and leaves with his swinging walk.

No need to interrogate Warszawski, he's an old gossip.

"Jurek killed his sister, at her own request. They wanted to send her to the front, to a brothel for the soldiers. He owes his life to a miracle, like nearly everyone. He was fifteen. They lined up five boys of the same height, one behind the other so that they lined up exactly. That was how the commandant did target practice. The trick was to pierce all five hearts with one bullet, a sport that was very much in fashion at the time. But this kid didn't want to get shot. He left the line and stood in front of the commandant:

" 'Sir,' he said, 'I'm young, I want to live.'

"His answer was a slap, a slap that would have knocked an ox down. But Jurek didn't flinch, he looked the 'sharpshooter' right in the face.

" 'He's really made of iron, this rascal,' he said.

"He briskly pierced the remaining hearts and employed Jurek as his stable boy.

"The poor child," sighed the photographer, "what has he seen of the world? The ghetto, the camp, and the 'actions.' The commandant is his second father and the dwarf is his adoptive mother. What can you expect with such parents? Imagine, he's never been to the movies."

His life's dream is to be a cameraman. If one day God allows him to go home, he'll try his hand at it.

I listen distractedly. Another story is running through my head:

"Once upon a time there was an apprentice optician . . . and they killed him." End of story.

—

A second night of continuous shooting: They're liquidating the "politicals."

They were rounded up in town. Since yesterday they've been standing under our windows with their faces turned toward the wall. Motionless, they wait for the bullet in the back. Why don't they scatter, or attack the guard? What do they have to lose? Why wait? Why add humiliation to death? Play the "dogs'" game? Usurers: With every bullet they buy a thousand slow, lucid deaths. That's what infuriates me! They have neither a thousand hearts nor a thousand throats; they'll each have only one death, the butchers!

Nobody is snoring in the barracks; I'm not the only one listening for the breathing of those outside. Not a murmur. And suddenly my throat feels dry.

"They're thirsty . . ." I take our water jug, jump from the bunk, run to the window, and open it carefully. "Wollen sie Wasser?"[1] I ask very quietly.

I can't make out any features in the darkness, just the negative movement of a head raised toward the window. I need to close it again right away, don't I know that it's forbidden to approach them? Yes, I know! But I don't care, I really don't care; in the space of a second I'm free, almost euphoric. I straighten up in the window opening. If they want to shoot, this is the time! But nothing moves, and I go back to bed almost disappointed.

I've barely gotten back in when it starts, and the bunks tremble along with us, as if they were machine-gunning the barracks. I tremble like everyone else, I

[1] Do you want some water?

barely manage to reassure myself: I'm alive. Not a whimper, not a murmur. Only the bursts of gunfire and the silent dazzlement of all those who are still breathing.

When toward dawn we hear a real cry, it almost revives us and we rush to the windows.

A nearly naked body is lying in front of the barracks. A woman SS is riding a bicycle over it. The body is moving. At one point the bloody head rises, but the young guard standing to the side pushes it back down with his boot so that his lively friend can continue her game. When she passes in front of us I stare at her closely; she's very young, her cheeks are aflame, she's giggling hysterically.

The bicycle . . . That wide adolescent mouth with its big flat teeth, that continuous giggling . . . I'm afraid they'll never stop rolling through my head, for as long as I still have one.

—

The terrible name comes up more and more often: Auschwitz.

The faces at roll call are ashen. One directive replaces another, a new one drives out the last.

People murmur that the railroad cars are ready.

People murmur that they won't have time to bother with us; that they'll always have time for that; that

Madame Potrez, the dwarf, has been liquidated . . . she knew too much. The commandant is evacuating his villa. The gallant gentleman let his accomplice go first. So he isn't as "obtuse" as all that. According to the photographer, this is just a rumor, because he would never for anything in the world deprive himself of the spectacle: What a beautiful hanging that would be!

Konhauser, in a rotten humor, demands imperiously that I burn my notebooks.

"I have."

I lie without batting an eye.

The "council of three" meets on my bunk, and although she's outnumbered two to one, the sculptress ends up taking my two notebooks away from me (Sophie and I are of the opinion that we should bury them at Plaszow). The discussion continues into the wee hours. Then, worn out by my resistance, which is at bottom not very sincere, I turn over my two notebooks and all the risks, left, right, and center.

I might never have understood her insistence without my adventure of last night: to "choose" in this slaughterhouse, to distinguish one's self, to give meaning to one's death.

What does it matter?

Why do people care about their tombstones?

Why did I take up my notebooks once again?

—

Auschwitz. Every word is made up of letters. Grammar.

In this huge crypt, there are once again too many of us. Ten or more are stacked up in a space that at Plaszow was occupied by three of us: Sophie, the sculptress, and me.

Sophie is alive. I thought I saw her as I got down from the train. Her short silhouette emerged one time from the crowd. Too weary to look for her.

The "council of three" . . . it won't meet again. The principal member has deserted. She slipped away, the wicked girl, at the last moment, she who was so proud of her country-girl strength! For three days she sheltered me like a baby. With her bony arms she made a rampart around me, protected me from the avalanche of other bodies. With exasperating stubbornness she revived me each time I was going to abandon the exhausting fight for air, and brought me back to the fetid heat. One time when I almost passed out, she made a path, pushed back the dead and living bodies, and managed to drag me to the wall of the car to make me breathe through the joints.

"Breathe," she ordered, pushing my face against a crack.

Someone relieved herself on me. I started howling.

She calmed me down. It's suicide, you mustn't waste your strength; she who didn't spare herself, who acted as if she had a hundred lives! The faker! Toward the end she was silent. But I have only a very confused memory of those hours; we were jumbled together, dead and living in a single stinking mass. I remember, though, that toward morning she sat up and started unlacing her shoes.

"What are you doing?" I groaned.

Some people grumbled because when she bent over she made the whole edifice of bodies sway, and it took a moment for the equilibrium of all those intertwined limbs to reestablish itself.

"Before it's too late," she said.

I didn't understand until later, when the door of the car opened and she didn't move. I called to her, I touched her: She was still warm. With her head resting on another body, she looked as if she had simply fallen asleep—and perhaps with a reassuring thought—her expression the same as when she was asleep on the bunk: peaceful.

"Before it's too late." She was thinking of the notebooks hidden in her boots! So she knew. She was afraid that when we arrived I wouldn't have time to retrieve them. That was what she was worrying about as she died. With the last of her strength she unlaced her shoes.

While the car emptied I had time to take her shoes off, retrieve and hide my notebooks, and look at her one more time. The memory is not depressing—on the contrary. For the first time I looked at death without fear, as if that face had taken it away.

—

I don't trust the mattress as a hiding place! Following established custom at Auschwitz, they're always chasing us out of the barracks. Fortunately the two doors of this terrible tunnel remain open during the cleaning, and our new "trainer," the beautiful Gise with the black hair and the depraved smile, can't ride her whip like witches ride their brooms. When she doesn't manage to hit anyone, she strikes in the air. That's how she sweeps through the barracks, several times a day. At her heels is a pack of little "trainers," horse breakers on a rampage; while Solange, the head of the barracks—a blond, pink, indolent doll—withdraws into her private cubicle and yawns under her blanket. You can see her clearly from our bed, every time the door of the cubicle opens (which happens often during the night, for detainees and their guards in turn); but seeing her at the morning roll call with her porcelain face, in her freshly pressed blouse, I wonder whether I haven't been imagining things. With her little plump hands she touches each of us as she counts us, but her colorless eyes rarely stop on anyone—which may be for the best, because she seems strangely lacking in a "gaze." And that makes you uneasy, sort of like having a blind person "stare" at you.

The first morning, she stopped not far from me to ask where we came from.

"From Plaszow," we answer in unison.

At that she raises her eyebrows. Her surprise makes her look almost animated; she runs off and immediately returns with Gise.

"You've been in this camp before?"

"Not in this one, in another one."

"I mean in Auschwitz?"

"Yes, and they brought us back," responds the chorus.

"Was it a big transport?"

"Around ten thousand."

The two women look at each other. And in the silence I hear a familiar voice, a firm, intelligent voice, that of Alice.

I turn around. She's no longer blond. Beneath her shining skull, her features are drawn. Even like this, without her crowning glory, she has kept something of her former dash. Where has her cousin gone?

"If you'd be good enough to tell us how many of us are here . . ."

"In my barracks, seven hundred," Solange answers readily, "and eight or nine hundred scattered among the others."

There's a silence. Konhauser, Warszawski, Sonia? I've always thought of them as neighbors whom I'll meet again one day or another on the Lagerstrasse. Isn't that how I met Sophie? Sonia with her head shaved! Lord, with her "bad temper" and her habit of laughing at herself until she cried. I don't have the patience to wait until the two Slovak women finish their incomprehensible dialogue.

"May we know what camp the others are in?"

Their talking prevents them from hearing me. I repeat my question. Gise, the brunette, turns around irritated.

"They're in Camp H," she says. "You don't know how lucky you are to be here!"

Solange gives us her rather dead smile. (There are creatures who should be forbidden to smile.)

—

We're in Camp B, so there are seven from here to Camp H. And after that? How many camps are there, here, each bigger than the one at Plaszow? More depressing, too. The distances, the barracks, the sky, the air, even the face and the lovers of Solange, the *Blokowa*. Yet the soup is more plentiful, and there's no question of work. I can squat down anywhere with my papers and not attract anyone's attention. I have a spot under the eaves that I share with the crows. Sometimes we stare at one another in silence for a long time. Is it my immobility that attracts them, or the fact that I'm small, quiet, and almost as black as they are? I write little, and with difficulty. Thinking makes me tired. I snooze sitting up. That's how I spend my time, from roll call till the soup distribution, from the soup distribution till the bread distribution. For how long? No idea! Nothing, for that matter, is as important as it was at Plaszow. Not even my "testimony"? More and more, it's a sort of obligation that the sculptress left me when she slipped away— and that I face up to halfheartedly when I'm not too tired.

People say it's the large doses of "bromide" that they put in the soup. Possible.

—

I dozed off in my usual spot. When I opened my eyes Sophie was sitting nearby. We often sit like this and take turns dozing.

"The wind here always smells like smoke, have you noticed?"

"Yes," I said. "Because of the crematorium."

"They're burning trash."

192 / Ana Novac

"They're also burning the dead. You remember, when we arrived the sky was red for two days . . ."

"That's normal. There must be a lot of demises in a place like this. What else could they do with them?"

And I burst out laughing.

"What's got into you?"

"There are a lot of 'demises' in a place like this."

"That's right," she says, "it's too abnormal to be serious. Isn't that so?"

"Why don't we get some sleep?"

———

An eternity since I've written. I no longer count the days. Since long ago and far away, I'm tired . . .

The "imps," I knew them before the great fatigue. One day they literally jumped me on the Lagerstrasse, especially one of them, the biggest (it turned out later that she was the youngest). One thing is certain: She's the head of the family, the most decisive, the most dynamic, which clashes with her sentimental nature; she has a gift of gab, a face like a fox, and a habit (rather annoying) of weeping for the slightest reason, if only because her glasses are always fogged. They were fogged when she jumped me. She hurriedly wiped them on her dirty dress.

"This is my sister," she hiccups, which isn't difficult to guess. It's as if she were thrusting her double at me, although the sister looks nothing like a fox. She looks more like an owl: big, round, bulging eyes, a pouting mouth, a puffy face, and all of it reflecting an indescribable apprehensiveness. A nestling fledged before its time, old and haggard. She used to give English lessons, which enabled her to provide for the needs of her whole family and send her younger sister to college.

They wear the same black-rimmed glasses, the same black rags hang on their backs, and they seem to be possessed by the same black anguish. All this doubled misery seems infinitely preposterous. They talk to me as if I were an old acquaintance. They take turns thanking me endlessly. In their enthusiasm they don't notice my stupefaction.

I try to think, I rack my brain: Where have I met these two specimens? Two pairs of dark-rimmed glasses. "The storm," I cry. Suddenly the flood of thanks stops. They're taken aback by the idea that I could have forgotten them.

It was a real hurricane; shivering in the depot, wrapped in our blankets, we had locked the door for fear that a gust of wind would tear it off. Several times it seemed to me that someone was knocking. The wind? I ran to the window: Two nearly naked skeletons, two pairs of glasses circled in black stared at me. The rain kept me from seeing any more. "Something warm," wailed a small voice made ghostly by the storm.

"They've escaped from the hill," I said to myself. "I don't have time to look for anything!" I quickly took off the sweater that Frau Reich had given me. I grabbed the first piece of clothing that came to hand, which was a little checked jacket that the indifferent Vania wouldn't spend much time looking for. I tossed both through the window to them. That was all.

After the memorable moment when they jumped me, the two sisters visited me every day. Their insistent friendship may have shortened my "testimony," but it also served as an excuse to be idle without remorse. One time they found me in a rotten mood. There had been a "mistake" in the kitchen; on the pretext that there wasn't enough soup for the whole barracks, the Stubendiensts had shared it among themselves.

"Come with us," suggested one of them (the prof). "We always get double rations."

"How?"

"Very simple, haven't you ever thought of it? You get in line in front of another barracks. Little by little you pass yourself off as one of them. That way you make sure you get a second helping every day."

"What if I get caught?"

"Don't be silly," the other one, the resourceful one, assured me. "They know us, we'll vouch for you!"

It worked once, and once again . . . five times. I ended up forgetting that I was "illegal." Otherwise I wouldn't have been able to look innocently at the unfamiliar Blokowa, a decent person who tried to defend me when, with a light heart and a full bowl, I almost ran into the arms of Gise.

"What are you doing here?" she asked, her face already lighting up with what she was going to do to me.

I looked at them in turn, her and the Blokowa, as if I didn't understand; I smiled, at a loss for words, ready to forgive her this little misunderstanding. The Blokowa said something to her in Slovak and an uncertain disappointment appeared on her face when she looked at me again. I may have returned her look too resolutely, because suddenly an evil smile revealed her sparkling teeth. She grabbed me and dragged me in front of the soup pot. "Does anyone know this girl?" she asked, peering at the ranks. The two sisters were in front. My pleading look met four blank windows. They had their eyes closed.

I remember that the first slap hurt. But the second one, I was expecting it. I started to smile, and without taking my eyes off Gise, I whacked her one, and then another . . . Silence! I heard the blows, sharp and magnificent. A divine calm came over me. As if that movement and that sensation were what I had been waiting for all my life. Apparently the smile lingered on my swollen lips even after she had roughed me up with the help of a half-dozen Stubendiensts. When Solange arrived with the guard, I was lying in the dust with a terrible pain in my stomach, but unfortunately conscious. I heard the "porcelain" woman, who had been called out in the middle of her siesta, ask in a disgusted tone, "What do we do with her?"

The German poked me several times with the toe of his boot. I was alive. Disappointed, he poked me harder. (They must have disturbed him, too, in the middle of digesting his meal.)

"Do what you want with her."

And he abandoned me to my fate.

I stayed on my knees in the middle of the Appel-platz for two hours, with a brick in each raised hand. Every time my elbow would bend, Gise, who never took her eyes off me, straightened my arms, and from time to time she leaned down to peer at my face. Toward the end my lips were cracked and so swollen that I could barely manage to whisper: "Water!" She leaned down again: "Shit!" she said, with an almost friendly expression.

A long story. But not mine. For two hours I was nothing but arms. Then I became myself again in an instant and the rest vanished.

I also remember that when they tried to take the bricks from my hands, they had to insist for a long time, my fingers were welded to them. My arms fell stiff, and it took a great effort to stretch out my legs. Yet during every second of those two hours I had only one feeling: *I can't take any more.*

Finally my bed. A neighbor on the bunk spent the night making me compresses. Her name is Ella, and she's not from our transport.

—

A boil under my arm. Infection due to a lack of cleanliness (although I wash as often as circumstances permit). At the dispensary the Hungarian woman doctor drained it for me this morning. I howled.

"Aren't you ashamed?" she said. "Save your tears!"

She knows my parents. She vacationed with them in Prague.

"Is your father still as high-strung?"

The funny question made her laugh. Suddenly her face brightened, and mine, too, because I knew what came next. I'm used to seeing people light up when they speak of her.

"Your mother is delightful! And so young!"

"Very young," I said, blushing.

I walked down the Lagerstrasse with a lively step, filled with a happiness I had forgotten. For a few moments I was once again the child of a delightful creature.

—

I was going to get my dressing changed. The Block-sperre caught me on the way there. I was very close to the dispensary, and I didn't want to turn back. A big red ambulance was waiting at the entrance. Impossible to get by. An officer wearing the insignia of the medical corps stopped me.

"Where are you going?"

I showed him the dressing. He unwrapped it carefully and looked at the sore. He had a delicate touch.

"Have you had that before?"

"Never in my life."

"How do you know German?"

"My mother is originally from Bremen."

"I see," he said, looking at me attentively with his black eyes.

I had already seen that face somewhere—tanned, thin, exotic. The "tribal chief" . . . The circle of naked women under the stars, and the officer who directed the dance with his index finger.

"Come with me!"

My heart began to pound.

"Where?"

"To a big hospital. We need to take good care of that."

"But I feel fine!"

I smiled. For some time my face had been disconnected from what was upsetting my bowels (a surge of diarrhea, which I also mastered). I saw the woman doctor on the doorstep. Had she heard those last words? She began to explain, using lots of technical terms, that my sore was not contagious, as it appeared at first sight. She guaranteed it. Then without waiting for an opinion from her "colleague," who seemed to hesitate, she pushed me into an empty ward.

I heard footsteps, moans, doors creaking. One of the patients wanted to bring her blanket, but they took it away from her. "My bowl," someone cried.

"Quickly, quickly. You won't need anything!" urged the familiar voice.

The engine started and they left.

The woman doctor came in.

"You ought to be . . ." But she didn't manage to finish the sentence, and flopped down on one of the beds.

"Where are they taking them?"

Maybe she didn't hear me. She stared at me in a tired way, like the Polish women at the depot used to do.

"I'm going to give you a little tincture of iodine and some dressings. I don't want to see you here again."

—

Ella finds me on the mattress. I say that I'm not going to get my dressing changed anymore, that I think funny things are going on and it's better not to be sick in this camp.

"Didn't you know? They cremate them. Calm down, not alive! They put them through the gas chamber first."

"Are you sure?"

"Everyone here might as well be sick!"

I sit up and make her continue, looking at her without flinching. Even though deep inside I'd prefer that she shut up, like the doctor. It's too late.

"Before you arrived from Plaszow, we, the old ones who are here now, were in Camp C. In B there were Czech families, men, women, children, all together . . . They had gotten to keep their clothes and their hair. We often chatted. They received parcels. They threw us chocolate bars and packages of cheese across the barbed wire. We envied them madly. One night we were awakened by shouts. We were worried; the Slovaks filled our heads with stories. In the morning the Czech camp was empty. The Blokowa was sobbing, the Slovaks' eyes were puffy. I found out later that they had known in advance what day the Czechs would be evacuated. They generally get rid of the 'old' prisoners every six months. Out of twenty thousand people who were brought in '42, all that remained were those three thousand; it was their turn that night, because six months had just gone by."

"Did they know it?"

"They suspected. But they hoped! It depended on the news from the front."

She was silent. Then after a moment: "Do you believe in God?"

"I don't know," I said. "And you?"

"Neither do I."

We sighed.

"There must be something, destiny or some trick like that," she said after a while.

"But what if there's nothing? Nothing but a bunch of questions!"

She didn't answer. We were silent, stretched out side by side.

"Are you asleep?" Ella asked.

"No."

"Have you ever thought about the electrified wire?"

"No, have you?"

"I'm scared."

"Think about it. Are you scared of having to go through a rough moment, or of no longer existing?"

"Of not understanding," she said after some thought.

———

Tattooing. They printed small numbers on the back of my left arm. I owe a debt of gratitude to the Slovak who worked in our line, skillfully and twice as fast as her colleague. Oh! The poor things who fell into the hands of that amateur! For the rest of their lives they'll have a big purple mark on the wrist. To say nothing of the fact that they're still there, shivering in an interminable line, while we, the lucky ones, have taken all the places in the latrines.

The latrines! Nothing like the ones at Plaszow. We call them the "club," and for good reason, because it's an international center, the most extraordinary one ever. It was there that I first met French people, two Chinese (both one-armed), Greeks, Dutch, Belgians, Spaniards, Poles, Russians, men and women jostling for the double row of "seats" that run the length of the building, which is huge like all the barracks here.

Once the roll call is over, there's an assault. Picture it: five or ten thousand people trying to get through the same door!

If only we were just shoved from behind! But what awaits us in front is worse: the excrement bucket. The "dragon of the W.C." is a fiendishly determined person. She's the one who hauls the excrement, in wheeled barrels, to drainage channels (?) or labs (?). She's usually standing on the latrines, legs apart, with the bucket filled to the brim and ready to slosh. Just one drop and everyone starts backing up—shoving—and yelling in every language, even Chinese . . .

The fact that I've escaped from the double pressure of the crap and the crowd every day can't be explained. It borders on the supernatural. But it's no picnic for the "dragon," either; she barely has time to catch her breath when a crowd is already pouring in through the other entrance, so that she no longer knows which way to "go" with the crap. This sometimes lasts for hours, and has its Homeric aspect. Another advantage: You get warm. And when you've finally won a place in the stinking heat, the air outside has become milder.

A dialogue that I overheard this morning; a man and a woman, both Hungarian, squatting side by side over the holes:

Woman: The air is unbreathable.

Man: Mustn't complain, the cold is worse.

Woman: It's easier to take than the stink.

Man: Then why don't you stay outside?

Woman: That's my business.

Man (after a long pause, conciliatory): In the morning it's Siberia, at noon it's Africa. Where is this damned place? I've never heard of it.

Woman: I haven't, either. Is it still August?

Man: Yes, I think so. Imagine what winter will be like!

The woman sighs.

Man (with renewed enthusiasm): No matter what

you say, the cold is worse. The stink, you manage to get used to it after a fashion.

Woman (resigned): Are you Transylvanian?

Man: Yes, from Ermihalyfalva. Permit me to introduce myself: Counselor Keresztesz, Attorney at Law.

Sometimes I try to catch snatches of the conversations that swirl around me, snatches of languages that I'll never speak, countries where I'll never set foot. All the roads that crisscross in these latrines: Paris, Moscow, Athens—Europe! In tatters, stripped, rejected, but it's here. It's like traveling at a dizzying speed in a vehicle that never stops. A frustrating, exhausting voyage, but I travel nevertheless, in these funny johns.

—

P.S.: I almost forgot: According to rumor, a tattoo is life insurance for one or two months. My number is A17,587. The Slovak first drew it in ink, then with the needle from a syringe she went over each number. It was like someone was giving me uninterrupted shots for several minutes. Painful, but bearable, more so than the fear. I switched my place in line several times, and when it was my turn I was nauseated. I, who slapped Gise and was thrown, or nearly, into the gas chamber—I really don't know what I'll answer, if the time should come, to the question "Were you brave?"

It started yesterday: Someone stole my shoes. When I got down from the bunk they weren't there anymore.

Insane with rage, I stomped around like Gise. ("Zählappel, you bitches!" she roars. "Are you waiting for me to pull you out of bed?" She strikes blindly. Except me! She knows my bed. On days when she misses me I hide during roll call, but she always ends up ferreting me out, the vile thing!)

I pound my head against the bed and demand my shoes, screaming.

"Be reasonable," poor Ella urges me.

She doesn't seem to notice that there are days when reason itself, nature, the universe, is unreasonable.

That's just the beginning. I've hardly left the barracks when my bare foot goes up to the ankle in a puddle. It's pouring rain, for the first time since we arrived at Auschwitz. The roll call is longer than usual. No question of getting into the "club" on a day like this. Ella and I take cover under the eaves. We rub each other's backs. No use. I have a roaring fever, but it's out of the question to miss tomorrow's roll call, or to ask Solange for an aspirin. I spend the day and night sweating between two blankets. I'm staggering, but on my feet. Ella has gotten me some funny boats, Dutch sabots (perhaps they came from our former depot at Plaszow). I drag my "barges" as well as I can in the mud (it's still raining); I have to stop and empty them constantly. Needless to add that I'm a source of constant hilarity; I spread mirth as I pass by—which is better than spreading a cold or the runs, after all. Laughter! I can already see the civilians' faces when I tell them, "I've never seen so much joking as in the camp."

Maybe it's hysterical, like at funerals. It's also true that we don't have any choice, because tears are the first thing to dry up. We all look like undignified widows—no, more like wandering bands of orphans, stricken with crazy laughter. People constantly commiserate with me while convulsed with laughter, assuring me that once the mud freezes I'll be able to take up cross-country skiing and other winter sports.

—

As I said, it was just the beginning. The barges have a use that no one thought of (imagination has its limits!). This morning when I got down, my foot sank into a soft mass. I stood there frozen, thunderstruck, stunned. A filthy bitch who didn't make it to the johns. I, alas, am the only one who knows that the filthy bitch wasn't me. One foot in the crap and the other in the air, speechless, I stink beyond words.

"Ugh," they holler from all sides. "A big girl like you! Aren't you ashamed?"

But nobody dares come near me. I don't respond. What can I say? Ella isn't around. I hop to the washroom. There's no water; this last blow finishes me off. It isn't the first time that I've been finished off and had the worst behind me; suddenly I find myself beyond the worst, beyond death, in the absolute nothingness where I'm finally untouchable! (Stinking or not, it's no longer my problem!)

———

"Where are you from?" a Frenchwoman asks me, in French, in the line for the water taps.

"From Transylvania."

She looks surprised and claims that in France they think that's a country of legend, a movie fantasy kingdom with princes and princesses with heavy accents— an accent like mine, in fact, and also like that of the girls in the Hungarian barracks.

I say that's understandable, since Transylvania is Hungarian at the moment, or at least it was three months ago, when they loaded us into the railroad car.

She gives me a skeptical look: Do I mean to say that our country is in the habit of molting?

I assure her that it's the pure truth, that we're constantly *molting*. That my grandfather was born in

Austro-Hungary, my father in Hungary, and I in Romania, without ever changing our town or our street.

"And you," she asks, "what are you?"

"Who can say? I dream in three languages, with an accent in every one. On my passport it says 'Jewish' in Hungarian, although I don't know a single word of 'Jewish'; before it was written in Romanian, and I have no idea what language it will be written in when I get back to my country. Maybe Norwegian or Turkish?"

She says that she's "Parisian," period, but since she adores accents, she's hoping to learn Italian just to have one.

It's her turn at the taps. She gets undressed, starts washing herself, asks me to scrub her back; with an ingenious brush (a scrap of blanket wrapped around a small stick), she thoroughly cleans her teeth. She doesn't have any more hair on her head than the rest of us, but from it she gets a "tomboy" look that leaves us open-mouthed. That's not the last surprise in store for us—the way she does her sack (the same shapeless piece of cloth that flaps around all of us), adjusting it on her bones with a skill that borders on magic, she gives herself a sort-of-outfit that brings out "curves" she doesn't have. It's an almost chic figure that walks away with a light step, swinging her "hips." With her hooked nose and her lantern jaw, she isn't pretty. But all eyes are on her, dazzled. The person leaving the Waschraum is a *woman*.

Sophie finds me in a funny mood, puzzled and a little irritated.

"Isn't it bizarre that we know everything about them—their kings, their streets, and every tenth-rate scribbler—yet for them we're nonexistent, a 'country of legend'?"

"That's the fate of small peoples," says Sophie.

Personally, I think the fate of being Jewish is plenty for a Jew . . . But no, according to Sophie, the thing that makes the Jewish fate unique is that it isn't sufficient unto itself, but has to bear other fates and other calamities—Hungarian, Polish, Russian, etc.—in addition to its own! That's why we were expressly *chosen* by the Lord on High! Thank you, I observe, the Lord on High just needs to find Himself another "chosen people" and make His apologies to us. I'm not sure I'd accept them, for that matter. Sophie advises me to be "tolerant," because a person can be mistaken about everything. She adds, "You know what the Slovaks say about a Jew who's so fed up with being Jewish that he electrocutes himself: 'He was an anti-Semite.'"

—

The French women nearly killed their Blokowa, who had threatened them with the gas chamber. She's lying in her cubicle with a sore head, she can't even "report." She doesn't get to be in on things!

We went over there. The barracks was seething! The French women were out of control.

"What a morbid fantasy! People being gassed by the thousands, in Europe, in the twentieth century!"

What if I had a word with them about my encounter with a certain "ambulance," in Europe, in the twentieth century . . . I have no desire to get beaten up! Besides, their stubborn confidence in civilization, the century, and all that leaves me speechless—almost as much as their "tomboy look," their toothbrushes, and their artful femininity—the fact that they use their margarine to soothe their skin the way they use their minds to soothe their "morale." Unbeatable in the art of comforting their spirits, glossing over their doubts, swallowing nonsense so long as it's "positive." Their barracks is a real "anti-depression" center. They're always "organizing" things: meetings, discussions, concerts, recitals, etc. I rarely go over there, because "civilization" means nothing to me on days when the air smells like smoke and grilled meat, and in the face of their gigantic optimism I feel as helpless as a fly in a caramel custard.

I must point out that their "optimism" isn't restricted to this world, but goes beyond all limits, including those of my reason. Ella and I participated in one of these "experiments." We'll never know what to make of it, no doubt because of our "limitations." There were about twenty of us, with our palms placed on the table, fingers slightly spread so as to touch those of our neighbors to "close the circuit" and "let the current flow." "Is it flowing?" the mistress of ceremonies, who called herself a "medium," asked from time to time—a tanned person with feverish eyes and a low, barely audible voice, as if she were afraid of cutting the "current." She wore a shining barrette like a tiara, or an aura! She reminded me of Cleopatra in a silent film that I once saw. She seemed to be very experienced with the beyond, and spoke to her "contact" in a voice slightly louder than she used with the rest of us, but without ceremony, with the familiarity of an old acquaintance: "Dear spirit, please knock as many times as there are days until our liberation."

(Why not ask how many weeks, I thought, and let us be patient for a while?) The "contact" may have shared my opinion, because it made us wait. The "medium" spoke of "interference." Sometimes the line was "crowded." We brought our fingers closer together to strengthen the current, just in case. Was it the current or fatigue? My fingers felt like they had gone to sleep, my arms hurt, and everyone started fidgeting nervously and making the bench creak.

The medium had the tense look of someone waiting for an urgent telephone call. Meanwhile she had no trouble finding "reasons" for the delay. As if the beyond were a "switchboard," somewhere on the other side of the barbed wire, that might be undergoing a temporary outage.

"Think how many calls there are at this turning point in the war!"

"What turning point?"

I couldn't see who spoke, or identify the accent; maybe it was that of a spirit. The medium answered in her low but irritated voice that victory was only hours away and that "negative waves" were very poorly received "over there"; they only disturbed her "contact."

"Come on," Ella whispered to me, "she's crazy, let's get out of here."

At that moment we heard the knocks, one after the other, sharp, loud knocks: Made by the table? On the table? Under the table? The fact is that no one saw the table move, or anyone hidden under it, and the table was too heavy, it would have taken several people to budge it.

That leaves the *contact*.

We crowded around the "medium," who was beaming like an actress receiving congratulations after a remarkable performance.

We didn't say a word all the way to the barracks.

"You know," Ella said to me later, in the dark, "it might have been one of the Czechs 'evacuated' from Camp B who made the knocks. They were jokers."

———

The camp reeks of smoke. A transport of Italian women is supposed to be housed in our barracks.

They turn out to be Greeks from Rhodes, but what difference does that make? Italian or Greek! The main thing is: three hundred more to argue over blankets and space. It's no longer possible to turn over, except on command: "by the left flank" or "by the right flank"; "on your back" is now only a dream. With my stomach cramps! It's impossible to raise my knees a little. If I just try, there's groaning and grumbling from all sides.

Yet the enforced paralysis is easier to take than the constant coughing of the Rhodians wrenched from their Greek sunshine; they're declining and deteriorating very rapidly!

New people are still a sensation. We hope for news of the war. Most of them seem to know only two words in German, *essen*[1] and *schlafen*,[2] and claim, like the "spirits," that the end of the war is only a matter

[1] Eat.
[2] Sleep.

of days. As for the Rhodians, except for their own language, they speak only Turkish (or about a war with the Turks). The other war, the big one—you wonder whether they've even noticed it!

At roll call they remind you of ghosts dressed up for carnival. It seems that all these low-cut dresses, negligees, and cloaks came from the baggage that our people left at the Auschwitz railroad station—furs, evening gowns . . . "As if they were expecting you at Buckingham Palace." The old ones constantly poke fun at them. More than their rundown condition, which is only emphasized by their outlandish clothes (you can feel the breath of death cross the Appelplatz), it's their innocence that troubles us. Their childlike eyes are round, feverish, bewildered: "What's this all about? Why?"

Seeing the ghostly procession making its way to the barracks, we almost recoil. One of them, with the face of a tortured madonna, asks whether anyone among us speaks French.

I introduce myself.

She looks at me with dilated eyes. She feels she's the victim of a miscarriage of justice; she wants to see a judge at once, and demands a review of the trial.

What judge? What trial? I try to explain to them that we're all in the same fix, not convicted but simply *in the way* on this earth. A waste of effort! Impossible to drag them out of their hallucinatory state.

They were put on a boat, three weeks in the hold with no hygiene and almost no food. Fortunately their children and parents are somewhere safe. They want to join them, and right away! I'm supposed to explain all that to the "judge," and also the fact that they've never appeared before a tribunal, even as witnesses, that they added their names to the "Jewish lists" on the advice of the rabbi, because in their country Jews are Greeks like everyone else, except in the cemeteries.

"And tell the judge that shaving the heads of young girls is unnatural, outrageous," and that they're ready to forgive, but not until "justice is done."

I'm only interested in one thing: getting away. But no, first I have to watch a performance by Béa, the jester of the group. Difficult to say whether she's crying or laughing, the two sides of her face are unconnected. One eye winks and the other one weeps, and she reinforces the "effect" by swinging her hips in an exotic kimono whose sleeves she lets slide up to show the marks of the whip on her flaccid arms.

"Poor Béa, what a beautiful woman she was . . . what a woman!"

All this is expressed with gestures—rather comical—to amuse her companions. But not me! They all seem to take seriously my role as "guide" and interpreter with the "judge." I'm in the middle of a crowd that's dropped from another planet or another time, and I'm their "voice," their providence, their only hope on earth. I could die!

"There isn't any judge, dammit," I repeat, exasperated, but the "madonna" who claims to know French (she danced at Lyon during a tour) only understands what she wants to understand. And what she wants is for me to be her sister and for her mama to be my mama.

I say that I have my own mama, my own family.

She answers, "Thank you, you're very kind. I'll dance for you."

I know that these people are seriously demented, that I'm as far from kindness as they are from their island! Although having no experience in the matter, I could be wrong. The fact is that I've never had the slightest occasion to be kind—someone always shows up to be kind to me before I think about it. I seem to have a special gift for monopolizing all the available kindness, for getting myself into unthinkable jams, like slapping Gise, for example, losing my shoes, or stepping in poop, and I don't know what . . . a bit like I was always drowning. And suddenly here I am faced with three hundred half-drowned extraterrestrials in critical condition, with a need for kindness that would make a saint shudder. I shudder, too, on the one hand, but on the other hand I'm tempted; I have a taste for adventure, and then who knows,

maybe it's *now* or never? Ella, the latest one to overwhelm me with her kindness, has a fit when I an-
nounce that I'm going to spend some time with the
Rhodians. "They all have TB." I say that I'll turn the
other way if they cough, but she must have a great
need to dispense her kindness to me, because she
gets mad.

———

Three days and nights with my "protégées." They
adore me; I understand them so well! I spend all my
time devoting myself, giving myself body and soul.
And the more I give, the more I have to give! And the
more I dissolve into kindness, the more my heart
swells with joy. Sometimes I'm afraid it will leave my
chest, rush to heaven, and take its place at the right
hand of the Lord. How can I deny that I've lived
outside myself—unaware of my deeper nature—that
in my catacombs was buried an unsuspected saint, ne-
glected for trifles? And what isn't a "trifle," compared
to saintliness? And what pleasure could equal the in-
expressible sweetness of self-sacrifice? A shame
they're so rare, the people who are clever enough to
understand that giving of yourself is the most delightful, and also the most worthwhile, of all vocations! In
any event, I can say that kindness is the best thing

that's happened to me since I was born; if only I had
devoted myself to it sooner! If only it could last . . .

—

No, alas, it has its ups and downs like everything else.
I often want to slap my "protégées" (right now, for
example!).

I wonder whether rodents have a saint—if they do,
it isn't me! I've been enlightened about the mouse
that was nibbling my bread. It's Lucrèce, the dancer,
and her little sister, Lola; I caught them on the bunk.
When they noticed me they started fumbling in the
mattress. They had obviously hidden my bread there,
disgustingly chewed. They tried to distract me, but I
saw everything, I heard their excited whispering, the
ragged breathing of Lola (the epileptic), whom her
sister dragged along behind her. My bread was still
wet with their saliva. If only they would break off a
piece instead of slobbering on it! And their charade to
top it all off! Yesterday evening when I found my ration had been gotten into, Lucrèce showed me hers,
nibbled the same way; why don't I go after them? I
have to calm myself down . . . I dawdle . . . Disgusted by my indecision, I finally jump from my mattress. But I feel sick, my head spins just imagining
Lucrèce's olive face, her eyes ready to jump out of
their sockets with simulated indignation, and Lola's
gasps as she creates a fake "attack"!

But after all it's not too late, I can spare myself all that! What consoles me a little for my cowardice is how shabby I would look if I managed to overcome it.

Lucrèce is dancing between two barracks, in the dust. The Rhodians beat time with their sandals and drum with their hands.

I can hardly believe that this creature of the air, defying the laws of gravity with indescribable grace, is the same person who is a bread thief, vulgar, dirty, and hysterical; that Béa, animated and almost beautiful, is the same simpleton; or that Gise, smiling like an angel in a triptych, is the same sadist that we know.

Tomorrow the sadist may beat the simpleton unconscious. Tomorrow the Rhodians will once again shiver from the cold, again they'll huddle together during roll call, and the whip will disperse them again. Lucrèce will return to her sordid little tricks with my bread, and I'll fall prey to the same rage.

But today we had a moment of beauty. I hasten to make note of it on the spot, because the day is not yet over. And you never know with the "dogs," as Sonia would say. I don't know what to think about her, or even in what tense. Can I still use the present?

—

At my workplace (under the eaves) I found a Polish man, getting on in years. I didn't dare take out my notebook. I started asking him questions just to pass the time.

"How long have you been here?"

"Three years. I won't last much longer."

"Not doing well, your health?"

"I'm one of the old ones, I'm ripe."

He seems to be looking at my face to see the effect of his ambiguous words.

"Haven't you ever heard of Camp H?"

"Vaguely," I say, and immediately regret it.

He points his index finger toward the sky.

"The *Himmellager.* The *Himmelkommando*[1] is waiting for me."

If only he'd spare me his unpleasant laughter!

"Oh," I say. I lean against the wall to steady myself, because I understand him all too well.

"What's wrong?" asks the Pole, breathing in my face; I won't comment on his breath.

"Nothing," I say. "So long, thanks."

—

As the days go by, my memories from before, while not being lost, take disconcerting turns, especially at night. A Rhodian back and two shins are resting on me, and suddenly the whole edifice shakes, because

[1] Heavenly camp. Detachment of heavenly workers.

I'm shaking with laughter; I remember the dormitory of the Ursuline nuns, the triple-casement windows, the white beds placed a good distance apart. We were standing in that room, my father and I, with the mother superior, Clothilde. She must have noticed that my father seemed embarrassed, because when she looked at us her glasses seemed to have a mocking gleam.

"Mother, I hope you understand. Your institution is excellent from every point of view, but this dormitory . . . We've always made sure that our daughter had her own room. She's prone to the flu, she's a fragile child."

That's how I escaped boarding school. Poor Papa, if you could see your *fragile* child, who catches the flu so easily . . .

—

We don't talk about it. But during the Blocksperre nobody stays still. We wander through the overpopulated barracks. We're walking off our anxiety.

This morning I was peeking through the cracks in the locked door. I spotted the "ambulance." It had already passed us when I saw a "nude" running down the Lagerstrasse. Had she perhaps escaped through the window of the vehicle? She reminded me of Lola.

Lola, whom Lucrèce and I had accompanied to the dispensary.

Lucrèce talked to her yesterday. She says that her sister is doing better now that she's being taken care of; she has a bed to herself, and they're giving her shots.

The car stopped. They must have caught the fugitive. I didn't see anything, I just heard a cry, and almost at once the frantic voice of Lucrèce behind me. I'd have been amazed if she had recognized her sister. Myself, I wasn't sure.

"What do you think?" she asked, plunging her disturbing eyes into mine. "If I give up dancing, if I make a vow to God, will my Lola get well?"

"I don't know," I said. "Maybe it's by dancing that you'll touch Him the most."

She squatted on the floor, closed her eyes, and smiled: "In Rome I danced for the *Duce*. I was only thirteen."

———

Lucrèce: an earthquake. She's been out of control since this morning. Her wiry body spews suffering with startling force. It can't contain it, you'd say. If only she could relax for a second! But she doesn't dare. When she feels herself weakening, she shakes herself and starts again stronger than before, as if she had to make up for lost time.

It's possible that suffering didn't figure in the "original" plan. Otherwise we might have inherited some abilities or instincts that would enable us to deal with it better! Like with work! It's not fair; only an indifferent or indecent nature could have created such terrible trials for such inadequate strengths.

P.S.: I wrote all that under the eaves. A messenger from the barracks arrived to tell me that Lucrèce had gone to look for Lola. Impossible to hold her back. She approached some SS, offering to dance for them, to do anything as long as they would take her to her sister. One of them gave her a punch in the stomach, and she got back to the barracks bent over double. Now she's in bed, with her eyes open, playing deafmute.

Finally she acknowledges me. She allows me to share a sorrow that's certainly beyond me. Although I no longer know what to think of myself—except that I have more resources than I thought! As if under my skin there slumbered a mother hen, one of those patient, obliging people who do the shopping with heavy baskets and a worried look. Fussing over my incredible "family." Carrying the anguish of others (three hundred others) relieves me of my own. I've never felt lighter.

—

More "family worries": My "children" have cut apart several blankets! They appear at roll call all bundled up. "It's cold," they explain to a speechless Solange. The verdict: Stay on their knees during roll call for the next four days; no food: two days.

Roll call reminds you of a synagogue on Yom Kippur. Gise is resplendent. Her whip is no longer idle; the blows and the moans follow one another without interruption. These poor things haven't yet learned to limit their losses.

In the evening they don't even have any voices left. They crane their necks toward me! Their eyes are like those of sick animals. I go look for Solange.

"I see," she says, "you have too much to eat. It won't do you any harm to go on a diet."

She listens to me without moving—her words seem to trickle from between lips that I don't see move, any more than her porcelain face. Like chatting with a ventriloquist.

I don't dare speak to the guard. I'm afraid of running into one of the Blokowa's nocturnal visitors. That only leaves the Sphinx, Käthe, the camp commandant. On the rare occasions when she appears at roll call, her Amazon size seems to obscure everything else; this Valkyrie is the one I have to approach. I take my time. She doesn't waste her energy, she saunters. Which makes my job easier. She stops in front of the soup pots on their way to the kitchens, tastes the soup, and mechanically slaps the two girls within reach. She's impatient with the ones who huddle together against the cold, and separates some of them as she goes by, murmuring in her outlandish dialect something like "Junge Leute."[1] Young people shouldn't shiver; apparently that's a principle that she believes in . . . It's incomprehensible: Why does this Juno dressed in a heavy sweater (just by chance, supposedly!) insist on toughening us up before she sends us to the gas chamber? Yet the way she tastes the soup gives me some courage, and I plant myself in front of her and stammer, "Excuse me," or "Bitte . . . ," I don't remember what.

"Huh?" she inquires, without seeming surprised, wrinkling her nose. In a few words I outline for her the Rhodians' situation and the recent events.

She blinks her eyes, and her visible effort to follow me makes me suspect that she's a Swabian from back home. She only speaks their local dialect, like some of our maids, to whom we had to teach German.

She reminds me of someone. I end up being certain that the person she reminds me of is herself. She used to be called "Kati," and she worked for us as a nanny

[1] Young people.

for a while. Her skin was less rough, but her nearly white eyelashes haven't changed, nor her beautiful vulgar mouth with the strong gums.

She hears me out to the end, and the expression of concentration never leaves her face. Then without saying a word she turns on her heel and leaves. The terrifying question remains: Did she recognize me? Not impossible, because her departure was rather stormy. One day when my parents were away, she shut me up in the cellar (I no longer remember why). I yelled and the neighbors came and liberated me. "Kati" was promptly dismissed, which didn't seem to bother her too much; I remember her final words, which were sometimes quoted in the family: "That little pest, I've had it up to here with her. I leave her to you and I wish you lots of luck."

I definitely must not have been a "nanny's dream."

I'm so worked up that I have to go to the "club" and jostle for a while. Back at the barracks, I find my "children" transfigured: Käthe has disciplined Gise, in front of them. This evening, a double ration of soup. Eureka!

—

The past is like a buried city, isn't it? If just one stone emerges, the rest follows! The day before yesterday

Kati-Käthe, today Edith. It's been an eternity since I've run across a familiar face, except for Sophie. And now, suddenly, two in less than a week! Without reinforcement, the past can get worn away. At the moment it seems to be making a sign to me: "Remember!"

Dear old Edith! A cook! She owes her enviable position to what was the agony of her life: her weight. I was suddenly assailed on the Lagerstrasse, actually lifted off my feet and almost smothered, by a sort of eiderdown, a warm mass that I couldn't identify until I had managed to extract myself from its embrace, half suffocated. Beaming! Glowing! I would have thought I was dreaming if it hadn't been for the stream of questions washing over me. It's really her! Impatient, curious, impulsive, excessive in too many ways and with no sense of proportion. In the face of this commotion you're always on your guard, like facing an avalanche.

At the age of ten she already had lines on her forehead, the result of her stormy thoughts. For example, at the age of seven she forcibly enlightened me about the scandalous things that grown-ups do when they're out of your sight.

That happened in the orchard. I remember protesting violently. But she started over, with all the horrible details, about the "shameful" information she had just gleaned from the lips of the cleaning lady.

I almost gave in and admitted that horrors of that sort might exist, but I balked on one point: "Papa and Mama? Are you saying . . ."

She was. I sulked for several days, watching from the corner of my eye the two hypocrites who secretly engaged in unthinkable practices (indispensable to my birth, according to Edith). "Tell me," I asked my father, "is it true that you had something to do with bringing me into the world?"

He turned pale and asked my mother in an inquisitorial tone, "Who does this child play with? Where does she come up with these things?"

I didn't see Edith again until years later. A victim of overfeeding used to treat a lung condition.

"Tell me," she began as soon as the door opened, "have I put on much weight?"

Her beautiful gray eyes asked for mercy.

———

Between questions she suddenly pulled back and ran her hands over her flannel dress (this same dress I'm wearing).

"I've gotten thinner, haven't I?" she asked with the old anxiety, and without waiting for my answer she let out a big laugh: "I must sound like an idiot!"

I don't remember what we said to each other. I just know that a respectful circle formed around us; a thin ray from her cook's halo shone on me. She squeezed my hand, constantly repeating, "What can I do for you?"

Caught unprepared, I didn't know what to say.

"You don't have any shoes?"

"Yes, but they're wooden, and I prefer to walk around barefoot."

"We'll see about that. Don't worry!"

I hadn't seen a mirror since Plaszow. But her agitation and some of her looks were as good as a mirror. Why should I be any different from the other "tramps" on their last legs that surround us? I'm probably worse, a disaster, for someone as blunt as she is not to say a word about it! She simply took off her flannel dress (she was wearing a Tyrolean-style dress under it); I put it on, there in the middle of the Lagerstrasse with a hundred of my counterparts watching, while she ran off. She came back in a few moments with a steaming bowl: meat, potatoes, and other delicacies from the bottom of the kettle. My awareness of everything evaporated—the tramps, Edith, it all dissolved in indescribable flavors.

We have a rendezvous at dawn, in front of the trash cans. (She warned me never to come near the kitchens, which are watched closely.) I hug myself in my flannel dress. How can I express the delight that my skin feels, under the caress of the soft fabric?

—

Hunting, around the kitchens.

They killed a young girl, two bullets fired from the watchtower. It's a dangerous sport, eating your fill. Bah!

That's not enough to stop me from showing up right after roll call in front of the trash cans, as agreed.

There are boards piled up behind our barracks. That's where I go with my bowl. I slip between two stacks. I have my hideout. The food or the silence, I don't know which I savor more. I'm no longer starving. I don't start until I'm settled in. Will the excitement leave me one day? Will I ever be able to look at a potato with indifference?

—

I don't know when I fell asleep. Nor do I remember waking up. I may have just been dreaming with my eyes open . . . about Jurek. He is (or was) a brute, but he was the only one to lay a hand on me, except for the doctor. What if I have a taste for brutes? What if he's right to think I'm "stuck up," a naive young thing who could leave this world in hopeless, ludicrous "purity"?

An idiot like me should have at least two lives, so she can enjoy in the second one what she daydreams in the first. Or are dreamers a hopeless species? Worse than alcoholics.

Now that I no longer have to think constantly about food, I wander down imaginary roads with imaginary guys, wearing imaginary outfits.

Imaginary embraces. If only they don't spoil the ones that I'll experience someday! To leave a world where you've barely begun to live! No, it's too stupid! All these lives, all these dreams suspended! I see them dragging through the ages, unfinished and unsatisfied.

—

The new convoys arrive wearing gorgeous sandals. I want a pair! And I'm in a position to bargain for some. Edith is ready to pay any price.

I show up with my sandals. She makes a face; she's no longer willing to pay!

"Are you cracked, or what?"

That's all she can find to say when I arrive wearing beautiful grass-green imitation lizards with thick wedge soles.

"You don't like them?"

"With that flannel dress? Do you think you're at a dance party?"

"If you have at least one nice thing, you can invent the rest!"

She launches into a long lecture: "It's summertime, but later, in the winter . . . with those high heels! Think about it!"

"They're not heels, they're wedge soles, the best thing for the rain. Besides, I like them!"

We part angry. In the afternoon she finds me again. She brings me a pair of spanking new boots, a little big. When I think about my barges! Even so, I can't forget those gorgeous imitation lizards. ("Neither can I," remarks Edith.)

—

Hanging by a thread . . . What a thread, good God, what a thread!

For fear that it will break, my thoughts hardly dare brush against it.

Today I met a Hungarian man at the "club." He knows what everyone knows: "The Russians are getting closer." Same story ever since Plaszow. The important thing is to leave Auschwitz, slip into a transport leaving for a work camp. You only have to glance across the barbed wire; in Camp C there are selections every day.

On the other side of the barbed wire several hundred naked women are turning in a circle, surrounded by SS and dogs. (Same show as when we first came to Auschwitz.)

I know some of them, in Camp C.

"My mother was selected. I would have liked to go with her, but the SS pushed me back. Where have they been taken?"

"I don't know," I say, "but you were better off staying."

"Hurry up and leave Auschwitz," the Hungarian insists. "In the work camps there aren't any selections."

"What is it, this camp?"

"It's a screening camp, a death camp. Present yourself for work at the first opportunity."

"I have a friend in the kitchen."

The Hungarian's face lights up.

"Great! I have a cousin who works there. Thérèse Sos. Would you ask your friend to tell her? The best thing would be to take her my bowl, if it isn't too much trouble."

"Why don't you go yourself?"

"I don't dare," he admits with disarming frankness.

I take his bowl from him. Heroes definitely don't hang out around the "club," nor on the Lagerstrasse. But to have the guts to admit his cowardice, that's really not too bad! As I take his bowl, he grabs my hands and thanks me, shamefaced: "A man is always more exposed."

Coming back with the two bowls, I hear a crack behind me and "it" almost grazes my side. I don't have time to be scared: Someone has shot at me from a watchtower.

Once again I receive my life as a gift. I may get used to it, in time.

The Hungarian takes his bowl, looking more dead than alive.

"You see!" he murmurs, deathly pale (he doesn't hide his relief). "Where would I be, Lord, if you hadn't taken my bowl!"

The next second he's up to his eyeballs in the soup.

"Masculine" courage and "feminine" fragility are for other people!

—

They've liquidated the "scabies block."

It was number 24, the most populous of all. Weeks ago they transferred everyone there who had a spot or sore on her body. They examined bellies with particular attention (and I thought scabies showed up between the fingers!).

The Blockälteste of the scabies barracks, the Polish woman Halima, is an almost legendary figure. She, too, has her contacts in the "beyond," which may be the source of her good humor—and that of the women in her barracks. Apparently most of them didn't really have scabies, they were faking. They showed up at the dispensary with all sorts of pimples and scrapes. The woman doctor did what she could. I wanted to speak to her about it on behalf of my "children," but before I was able to, they were simply taken away at roll call.

I have my place among the Hungarians. When I saw the procession trotting behind Solange, looking less "ghostly" than usual and with an almost lively step (some of them threw me kisses), they were on their way to join "the mamas and the babies," and they'll be back on the island for the picking season, like I *swore* to them a hundred times . . . I've lost three hundred children, without shedding a tear, and now I won't have to swear anymore. Last night they emptied number 24, the many fakers and the few, if any, with scabies.

Halima the "legendary" is crouched in front of the door of her barracks, crying. They're disinfecting.

It's number 19's turn, they say. Then ours? Solange won't cry.

—

The Germans' barracks has been bombed!

No other barracks was touched.

Lagersperre. We hug one another on the bunks. The same joyful commotion rises from the neighboring barracks. The Fritzes probably hear us, but they don't have time to bother with us. They have to deal with their dead. The disinfection scheduled for today has been postponed.

—

No more boxcars. We're riding on bench seats. Maybe the war has finally been won, because we're given blankets and tea. The windows aren't barred or nailed shut. I raise myself a little on tiptoe: It's a sort of fairyland that passes before my eyes. Except that my feet hurt; they've had to share space in my shoes with my notes (a six-mile hike to the station, every step a torture). Finally released but in a sorry state, my toes aching, my "work" crumpled as if it had come out of a trash can (or worse). I have a strong desire to toss it at the foot of one of these hundred-year-old trees.

Instead, I'm making a "report" of our trip in the margins of the newspaper I found in the toilets: the *Schlesische Volkzeitung.* We started out in front of the same door, with the same sign saying WASCHRAUM, with this difference: We were no longer "novices." Around twenty SS and the same number of Kapos, with whips, weren't able to make us budge. We didn't trust the sign—those "dubious" showers—we knew too much about them, you see!

Dig in your heels! So it's not just a figure of speech! I don't feel the blows; contrary to the tradition of condemned men in every genre, a film of my life does not roll in the minutes that I have left (like it does on the screen, where the guy in Sing-Sing walks to the electric chair while in a flashback a happy baby smiles at his mama). No baby, no mama, no flashback! My bowels still have top billing. The runs! Could that be the final sensation? I don't remember a single cry. The first sound reaches me when I'm in the shower, and it's a sort of rumble—perhaps from the water, which is spurting—that seems to come from far away, outside the walls.

After the scalding shower, outside there's another, icy one. We wait for morning—standing, soaked to the bone, shivering. Euphoric.

The sun finally rises with a certain pomp. And it's in front of the bath building in broad daylight that we make the *discovery:* We've spent the whole night in front of the crematorium. A low, nondescript building of red brick. "What's that for?" somebody asks one of the Kapos. He answers with an "eloquent" grimace, otherwise we might have taken it for the entrance to a bunker or a cellar. No odor, no smoke. No "atmosphere." Even when you know why these bricks were laid, they're just bricks, that's all.

The insignificance of the things and places that a

massacre leaves behind. No one breaks down. (Could
we all have amnesia?)

Miles of barbed wire, hopelessly alike: the same
nasty barracks, in the same order, the same ragged
crowd.

Imagine my surprise when I see, here by the crematorium and the disinfection hut, private houses with
curtains, little vegetable gardens, laundry drying on
lines, and on the benches in front of the houses,
women sitting with their kids! A little boy plays the
accordion, another drags a bike. They're civilians—
employees of the crematorium? In their spare time
they raise chickens and take care of their gardens.
Farther away, behind the buildings, are fruit trees and
perfectly straight lawns. These people seem to be settled in. Do they think they'll grow old and gray in this
place? The sun shines benevolently on this peaceful
colony. And this baby nursing intently was born here,
and this is where he'll go to kindergarten. An unknown woman is nursing her little one on the ashes of
one of my family, perhaps. Which doesn't diminish
the pleasure that I get from the sunshine, nor the
disturbing idea that I've avoided sorrow, that from the
beginning I've evaded and cheated by postponing
suffering in a cowardly way, adapting to it little by
little without letting it get close and grab me. Now it's
too late, I've compromised my mourning, forever sac-

rificed my right to it! Of course, I say to myself—
pitiful excuse—that I'm not the only one in this position. That if our suffering were equal to our misfortune, not one of us would still have her sanity. No, no
one fainted before this pile of bricks! Shit, am I re-
proaching myself for my *reason?* Is it my fault that it's
so hard to lose, even more so than life?

We're ready for the march, but we've only gone a
few steps when we have to stop for a procession that
passes in front of us for a good quarter of an hour,
flanked by SS with fixed bayonets. At their heels are a
pack of police dogs. Boots, striped uniforms. Under
the white scarves, faces leaden with fatigue, almost
interchangeable. It's the first time this has taken
shape before my eyes: "forced labor" in all its bleak
reality. Until now we've just been a disorderly bunch
of shiftless loafers.

"Anne!" The shout doesn't interrupt the noise of
the boots, but there's a stir among our group. The one
who cried out is feeling faint; she recognized her sister
in the ranks. But the line of boots, work shoes, and
dogs continues. Imagine Anne turning around, making a sign . . . a wave against the sea!

"She isn't even stopping!" screams the sister (discipline, we still haven't got the hang of it!).

We start walking. After so many miles of barracks,
and the village with the camp's employees, here we

are in the middle of a fairy story. Could this still be the camp? Although they're lifesize, the houses look like the ones you see at fairs, made of gingerbread. Trees with shining leaves and red apples, I've never seen any so big. Is it a set for an operetta? And as if it were the only thing missing, there suddenly appears a fantastic procession! *Die Vögelein im Walde.* Four majorettes move along a path, each carrying a different musical instrument. They approach two by two, and it's only when they get to me that I notice: Each pair is in fact one person doubled. Twins! Slender, blossoming, graceful; the only spot of color on each white costume is a yellow star. They're singing heartily: *Die Vögelein im Walde.* An older woman, thick-set and bony, walks in front carrying an accordion. She directs the little orchestra with great verve. On her chest is the same dark green triangle that Otto wore (the badge of a murderer).

—

I dreamed that we were no longer at Auschwitz! I hesitated a good while before I opened my eyes. Broad daylight. The train is stopped at the foot of the mountains, in a small station: Wiesau.

—

Before I forget: I've found out what it is with the twins. They're selected in the boxcars. They can keep their clothes, and they get three meals a day: the good life! In return, frequent blood samples are taken from them for experimental purposes. The question that preoccupies "the race": How can they double themselves in the womb?

—

Corn as far as the eye can see.

It brings tears to our rank of five! (We still have some!) It also reminds me of Sophie's words: "I don't have a feeling for nature." I must be lacking some feelings, too, because I didn't find time to say good-bye to her. And here I am walking along a wide road, bordered on both sides by plowed fields. No SS among our guards. Old gentlemen, grandfathers in uniform. They answer our questions, hurried and seemingly alarmed. That's how we must have looked at the Rhodians when they arrived. Although we don't look like a "carnival," they've given us the usual sack dresses. Bah! We must be a less-than-reassuring sight—although I'm sure they've seen others, at their age.

We've left behind us a real forest and a real street with real houses. I'm hardly surprised to see, at each green window of these little white houses with red roofs, the same faces with blond tresses and blue eyes. It must be our strange procession that draws them. Yet I have the impression that they've always been there

and will always be there, until the end of time, blond
and blue-eyed, as if they were part of the landscape.
The camp (if I dare call it that) awaits us in the
middle of a forest, and it, too, seems to have been cut
out of a picture book. We're the only thing that
clashes with this charming scenery; our shaven heads
turn in all directions, bewildered.

What could be worrying the three people waiting
for us at the entrance? A gentleman with graying tem-
ples and small, lively eyes above a big nose, with fat
cheeks, hearty, jovial, and red; his uniform, which
hasn't had time to be broken in or to adapt to his
plump figure, looks as new as his medals and his
camp, which still smells like household cleanser. But
there's no way to convey his perplexity! After looking
over the ranks, he speaks to a blond woman whose
sumptuous beauty also seems barely contained in her
uniform. They're talking in low voices when a second
German woman joins in. Next to the luxuriant
blonde, I had hardly noticed this mini-uniform. Yet
she seems to be the one who settles things, in her
little bird's voice. Finally the big man (who is undoubtedly our chief) stands facing the ranks, opens
his mouth, and then changes his mind as if he isn't
sure that we would understand the spoken word. The
little woman, who doesn't take her eyes off him, gives
him an encouraging smile as if to say, "Go ahead,

they're human beings." And after this unfortunate beginning, the fat man doesn't do badly. He begins by admitting that our appearance worried him at first. He knew, of course, that in the concentration camps we didn't enjoy impeccable conditions . . . (the ripple of laughter that runs through the ranks only stops him for a second). But the last thing he would have expected was that they would shave the heads of "ladies." He can see only one explanation: parasites, he concludes, blushing (this time no one laughs; we're no longer in the territory of the Reich, or else this character doesn't have all his marbles).

We're going to work in an earthenware plant. Our food, he warns us, is the responsibility of our employers; it will be a little less consistent the first few days, until the plant starts operating. He asks that we be patient, clean, and one thing that means more to him than anything else: that we tie around our heads the napkins that will be distributed right away; the sight of our baldness is unbearable to him! Then reflections on womankind and the place it occupies in his esteem, in spite of his age, which has taken away none of the respect that he feels for our sex. (No, we're in the Reich, but a Reich that's unrecognizable—courtly, gracious, a romantic little place.) Here we'll make earthenware in the peace of the Lord and mutual respect. The talkative little woman seems to endure the digressions of her superior with growing impatience. To our amazement she cuts him off. (Discipline isn't their strong point, either.) She starts chirping energetically; she announces that we'll have to wash every day, that there's hot water waiting for us in the washrooms. At ease. We're dismissed.

Four or five rooms in each barracks. Twenty bunks per room, and one person per bunk. ONE! With a blanket! A pillow! A spoon and a real earthenware plate! The soup is real consommé, the most delicious, and the clearest, that we've ever tasted in a camp.

I don't have time to choose a bunk where, overcome by all these exciting prospects, I can finally stretch out and calm down, when they're already calling us back.

They've forgotten the most important thing: choosing the Blockälteste and the "staff." Farewell to calm, happiness, hope, and relaxation. The icy shadow of Solange, Gise, and other bitches glides over this peaceful place. Except that they were already there waiting for us with their whips, and because of that there was never any question of equality between us. But to be under orders from someone who got off the same railroad car, shaven and starving like me! Oh, no! I protest in the name of all the derelicts, all the shaven heads. A complete waste of time. The assault has already begun; they shove excitedly, on the principle that if we have to have a chief anyway, it might as well be *me!*

The *Lagerführer* defends himself against this wild tide of ambition, which he has himself unleashed in his ignorance of how these "ladies" might think. The three of them barely manage to stand up to the assault. "Ich . . . Ich spreche deutsch,"[1] scream five hundred throats at once. Suddenly I recognize my own breathless voice in the chorus, and I shut up, dumbfounded. (I'm really too far gone to deprive myself of my sympathy.) I wait for the end of the match, sitting in the doorway, where Ella joins me. Difficult to predict a winner, because the "contestants" all seem on the verge of apoplexy, gasping, sweating, half out of their clothes.

The chief, probably to get it over with, grabs someone—just in time, she was ready to pass out—and makes her Lagerälteste. She looks like an escapee from the gas chamber. But once she has "triumphed," we witness a miraculous transformation. With her death's head beaming, dripping benevolence, she makes a small, regal gesture to the crowd (that would ruin the appetite of Death himself). The second is Sarika, the "pot licker." (One day Gise is supposed to have dragged her by the tongue out of the soup pot whose bottom she was licking.) Puffy with happiness

[1] Me, me! I speak German!

and tears, she's a country woman who's a little cracked from having kept her innocence too long. Lastly there's Tobie, a sturdy peasant woman from *Maramures*, with two little sisters in her care and the unquenchable vitality of the Falks.

You should have seen the Lagerführer congratulating them! The "pot licker" and the "death's head" accept the compliments with a sort of natural dignity as if the praise was theirs by divine right. The less fortunate who were sparring with them a moment ago hover around the new "chosen ones." Their servile and tormented smiles . . . (what a scream).

Barely an hour has gone by and already the new "dynasties," the new "courts" have formed, and the new intrigues, rivalries, etc.

I can't be in the same room as Ella. Their "majesties" are worried about "plots."

———

So this is Paradise! No work! No food! My teeth are just for decoration. Real camp soup is unknown here. Light soups of beans, sorrel, beets. If only they wouldn't put them through a food mill! And the bread! Laughable. If it weren't so fresh! It melts in the mouth like honey!

I'm taking a siesta on the lawn, beside the fence.

The silence of this early autumn is so soft, so romantic! Mountains are visible in the distance, and I wouldn't hesitate to trade them for a hard-boiled egg. A sidewalk in front of me. Under the fence I can make out old shoes, and an old broom sweeping up the dead leaves.

I have a mad desire to call out to her, "Hello, what did you have for breakfast?"

You can't see through the fence. Stretched out, I can see only sandals, bicycle wheels, and there's a shopping basket! The aroma of peaches and fresh bread, a hand holding them out to me. In such hallucinations the days drag by. Little by little I'm getting used to the fact that no one is guarding us.

The barbed wire, the endless roll calls, the Blocksperre, the breathless counts. And suddenly here I am beside a fence that I don't climb simply because I doubt that in this picturesque village I could find anyone willing to share his lunch with me.

How many facets does this nightmare have? What if History is a lunatic and we, the Jews, are his "madness"? A thought which doesn't prevent me from noticing that this is the second pot of soup to disappear into the Blockältestes' room. Sometimes, when one of the "courtesans" opens the door, familiar vapors tickle my nose, and my indignation matches my appetite.

—

Today crazy Sarika, with all her retinue, stopped at the door of our room.

"What, don't you stand up for the Blockälteste?"

We stood up.

We're not spared roll call, although they just count us as a formality. Only the verbal diarrhea of our chief justifies the ceremony. We stand for half an hour so that this would-be Cicero can have the pleasure of listening to himself! He says "Madame" to the two "reigning" shrews; he addresses himself in the same way to Tobie from Maramures, the "distinguished" washerwoman. The rest of us are his "children." He exhorts us to "be patient," as insistently as if we were in a position to refuse. I wonder how this masquerade will end up. If only he were as generous with the margarine as he is with his feelings!

And the earthenware plant? "The talks are proceeding." What talks? Earthenware! Nothing better to manufacture when their Kampf and their Reich are practically finished. But let them manufacture whatever they like! (A week from now I may have a full pot of soup and the Lagerführer may be standing in line with his bowl.)

—

Edith Berkovits. That name heads the list of those in our room. It's the name of the person in charge. Except for Szenttamas and us, no one will ever know that she is a girl of great rectitude. She carries out the distribution fairly, without favoring her mother and her sister.

That's why I would like for her name to escape oblivion.

—

In a death camp there's only one thing to do: save your skin. But once that's done, "arrangements" are possible. There are those who can look after themselves, and then there are the others! Me, I'm one of the others.

The Blockälteste, Pot Licker, finds me stretched out on my stomach. I'm writing. She stops, and her retinue along with her.

"What are you doing there?"

"You can see perfectly well!"

Indignation and indecision struggle on her flaming face. She isn't yet comfortable with her "rank"; her authority galvanizes and frightens her. How can she stop us from laughing behind her back, and erase that pot story from our heads?

She also knows she's supposed to do something to set an example on the spot, but what? As luck would have it, Tobie from Maramures has a less complex nature. She snatches my notes and gives me a hard smack. Gise herself couldn't have done better! What bothers me is that at the critical moment I can't stop my lips from trembling. Before I can regain my "sarcasm," Pot Licker and the washerwoman are already far away. One small consolation, nevertheless: I don't flinch. Barely an hour later Sarika, the old maid, comes back with my notes. Now that she doesn't have to defend her "rank," she falls back into her natural artlessness; she says that she knows how to write, she even has nice handwriting. Yet she's never thought of becoming a writer. Curious, isn't it?

"Maybe you'd be kind enough to write something about me, but without mentioning that I asked you to."

"Right now?"

She smiles, embarrassed.

"If possible . . ."

I come up with something on the spot:

You are sweet, Sarika, as a sky in spring
Shy violet, fragrance of another time . . .

I hesitate to give it to her; artlessness has to have its limits.

But the old bag beams through her tears and can't thank me enough.

"If only my poor mama could hear you . . . !"

Apparently she accosts everyone she meets.

"Have you heard the verse our writer made about me?"

My royalties: two extra helpings of soup! (Potato content, average.)

It was only a modest beginning.

Since then the whole barracks chases after rhymes. "Works" are dedicated to Tobie and to Death's Head. Someone has dubbed the latter "Queen of the Night." Someone else has composed an ode to the Lagerführer and won his big heart forever. Each verse ends with this refrain:

> *The Lagerführer, rah!*
> *He is our papá!*

We shouldn't give up on Papa's promises: A shipment of clothes has arrived. There's everything from overalls to overcoats. After an hour we're unrecognizable! It's the energetic little supervisor who's in charge of our "metamorphosis," at an implacable speed and without regard for our "feminine" sensibilities. Which leads to recriminations and acid remarks: "She has a date! That's why I'll be swimming all winter in these golf knickers."

Only a person who is terribly rushed or thoroughly stupid could come up with this mixture: a hunter-green cocktail dress—cut low and offering a plunging view of my collarbones—with an apple-green coat. Both spanking new. Which do nothing to brighten up the rings around my eyes or my gray complexion. According to Ella, I look like a racetrack in the mist.

Dressing up! Just yesterday it belonged to the realm of fantasy! And now that we're wearing the un-hoped-for sweaters, dresses, and coats, we can't stop grumbling, criticizing the color and the cut, cursing the supervisor and Papa. Obviously it isn't made to order, there are things to find fault with, except the one thing that no one breathes a word about (just writing it is heart-wrenching), which is that we don't look very good, and we can no longer tell ourselves that it's because of our tramps' get-ups.

Still, one of us is happy: Serène. She saw someone wearing her "civilian" coat, which she had deposited with the rest of her things when she arrived. She didn't have to pressure the new owner to get her to agree to an exchange. The lining is gone, it's thread-bare, a real poor person's coat! But it's HERS!

Days spent in excitement. An unforeseen event al-most made us forget "lunchtime": In a pocket someone found a magnifying mirror. Everyone wants to see herself close up, "magnified." Death's Head, too, in her fur-collared coat, waits to come face-to-face with her eye sockets.

Like the others, I wait. But I'm seized by a sudden coughing spell and have to stop; they take advantage of it to push me back. I give up, but even as I withdraw I can't turn away from this motley, effervescent crowd. These women don't look like tramps, nor like ordinary people in the street. It's as if a tribe arriving from another planet had disguised themselves in earth fashions. They run back and forth, examine one another and offer advice, yet nothing looks quite right.

The camp's two dressmakers are assaulted. At their wits' end, the poor things have no voices left to answer the endless questions; it's only when one of the "authorities" appears on the horizon that the shadow of a smile passes over the exhausted faces. All for nothing! The Blockältestes and even the minor dignitaries are able to choose their clothes: size, color, etc. Therefore the dressmakers, not having any hope of big customers, turn exhaustedly to the many waiting little ones.

As for my "greenery," it's no problem. The coat isn't bad, but the cocktail dress is the sort of thing that delights everyone I meet. I might be delighted, too, if I hadn't made a distressing discovery when I saw myself in a windowpane: Is it possible for your neck to get longer, at my age? On the other hand, my head seems to have gotten smaller. How could I not have noticed? I advise myself to avoid windows.

———

Some light on Papa's past, via Sarika. He was formerly a fish merchant and had a shop in town. I can see him clearly behind his counter, with his plump figure and his crafty eyes, his fat white hands holding the slippery merchandise. He's a "slippery" one himself. His eyes sometimes slip over us with a woebegone expression, like a grocer looking at tainted goods. He went bankrupt before the war. He was no longer at an age to distinguish himself at the front. He has always gotten mediocre assignments. This little camp is his first stroke of luck. Still, the situation is not good. He has three unmarried daughters (being unmarried herself, Sarika talks animatedly about it). Even pretty women can't look forward to anything but cripples or memories. The able-bodied men are "falling back flexibly and to their last breath." They've already abandoned Russia and are valiantly defending our Carpathians. All that's left as hope for happiness are wrecks and adolescents!

Even the blond supervisor wastes her opulent charms with pseudo-males: a puny little boy, is he even old enough to shave? The beautiful creature flushes scarlet when this half-pint appears on the other side of the fence.

Our Edith does her hair and nails. One time, after knocking at the door and getting no answer, she surprised them in a strange position: the little boy on the blonde's lap. *O tempora!*

—

More Finns! There are thirty-two of them, and it's the room next to ours that they've invaded. Mind you, these don't come from the far north—nothing to do with the descendants of the Vikings, fjords, and all that. They're called Finns because "fin" is how they pronounce the German word *von*. They're Maramures "Finns" (peasants like the sculptress). They swallow their consonants and draw out syllables forever (Maaaa, nuuuu). The treatment they inflict on our language is a bit reminiscent of the Huns. But the resemblance ends there. The Huns had their touchy honor, while there's nothing the Finns care less about.

One day they climbed the fence and ransacked a wagon loaded with sugar beets. Papa, who saw it all from the window of his office, called an assembly to let us know that we were the bitterest disappointment of his life and that the next day at dawn—no, that very night—he would send us back to Auschwitz. According to the rumors, Auschwitz has been freed—to say nothing of the fact that the margarine and vegetables he gets because of us are worth their weight in gold! Nevertheless we were in an awkward situation. Tobie the Finn threw murderous looks at her compatriots. She seemed ready to charge them and bite them like a dog. Papa was probably bluffing. Aren't we his "deal," his "stroke of luck"? But Pot Licker swears that she was the one who saved us, by falling on her knees in the middle of the roll call. She implored Papa to send her alone to her death. Up there on high she would find a way to draw God's attention to our camp (overwhelmed as He is, He must have lost track of us). I saw in Papa's eyes . . . two tears in the shape of fish.

The Finns were sentenced to a day without food. That was the day before yesterday. Result: Last evening they forced the door of the cellar. Loaded with potatoes, caught, unmasked—it takes more than that for them to lose their heads. Supposedly they found the door open; may their right hands wither, may they never see their homes again, if a single one of them touched it. These few potatoes, they picked them up on the stairs; it was probably the cooks who dropped them on their way up.

And since we're on the subject, here's a small sample of my own dealings with the Finns: One morning I was on duty, helping Edith with the cleaning. I was working on the beds when the door opened very cautiously and in the crack appeared a checked scarf, then furtive blue eyes, a snub nose, and finally the rest of Frimi, the head Finn, the "brain." She threw suspicious looks around her (I was crouched down between two beds, holding my breath). Sure that the coast was clear, she rushed to the shelf and took a cup. I stood up and confronted her—that's as red-handed as you can get, but not good enough for a "brain." To my consternation she was the one who started hollering first, raising a hue and cry: "You have the nerve to claim that this cup, you didn't swipe it from us? Bunch of thieves, phooey!" Before I could collect my wits, she ran to get the Blockälteste. The cup had disappeared from their place! Thirty-two Finns ready to swear on the salvation of their souls, may their right hands wither, and so on . . . They got the cup. Their right hands didn't wither; on the contrary, they used them to continue their shady activities.

The day without food was extended by one more, and in addition they were restricted to their room.

Since this morning they've been yelling without a break. A thin partition separates us.

"Why are they screaming?" I asked Edith.

"They're saying their prayers."

"But why screaming?"

"Just in case; on the off chance that the good Lord is busy elsewhere or born deaf!" Then with a disillusioned grimace: "I wouldn't give two cents for their faith; they eat pork, and they operate light switches and do business on Saturday like goyim."

She, Edith, would let both her hands be cut off rather than touch a knife on the Sabbath. How meticulously she removes every shred of meat from her soup! She observes all the fast days, major and minor, staggering sometimes, half fainting! Frankly, I think her "Supreme Being" gives her a hard time over trifles. I much prefer the Finns' Süsser Gott[1] who isn't a bit finicky or a stickler for formalities.

In the evening they ask him to protect their sleep, and they sleep like logs. In the morning they implore him to satisfy their hunger, and he closes his eyes to their raids and their stealing, and the Finns are satisfied. He's tolerance itself except on one point, and there he's immovable: loyalty. They squabble constantly, but don't misunderstand: When one of them's in a jam, thirty-one lionesses come running. They make all their "expeditions" together, address the Süsser Gott in chorus, and rigorously share the loot.

Here's a Finn story. It dates from my first stay at Auschwitz (before I started making notes). There

[1] Sweet God.

were two little Finns on the bunk. They made themselves equally insufferable.

One day I found one of them in tears.

"What's wrong?"

She sobbed harder. At the toilets she had eaten a piece of fatback, given to her by a Pole. I observed that she wouldn't go to hell for that.

"It isn't the fatback," she said, "the Süsser Gott will easily forgive me for that; but I didn't share it with my friend!"

Which left me speechless, because they fought day and night. We spent our lives separating them. A little while later there was a selection. The friend had a skin rash and they set her aside. The Finn with the fatback clung to her. The German lost patience and added her to the selection.

Our thirty-two Finns enjoy excellent health. Ten to one they aren't screaming themselves hoarse in vain: The Süsser Gott, who's just an old Finn, will get them home to Maramures in fine shape, every one of them.

—

The Kueppers factory. It's finally opening its doors. Papa announces it solemnly at roll call. He's wearing his white uniform, his two aides are there, and even Kurt, the male-for-lack-of-anything-better, is watching from the end of the terrace.

For once, Papa doesn't play the orator; nonetheless his performance is a resounding success. From his first words we're galvanized.

The manager of the Kueppers factory is asking for a hundred workers; they have to be people who are strong, well-mannered, diligent, etc.

Papa examines us with a worried eye; he knows what to expect from a crowd that he's compelled to keep starved, in view of harsh realities and all that! We're all on the alert, ready to pounce. But Papa isn't the novice who first greeted us. He finds the right words to cool our enthusiasm: "Those who push will eliminate themselves." He will personally choose those who are most worthy for this important task.

Is it because of my green coat, or my "well-mannered" look? In any case I find myself among the elect, already nearly worn out by excitement, hope, and expectation.

We leave in silence for the first job, we the hundred, the shock brigade of the Wiesau camp. From the door our chief addresses a few more encouraging words to us. Behind the fence his paternal smile and several hundred deeply disappointed looks follow us.

Breathtaking news circulates through the ranks. We

make the trip with wings on our feet, and don't notice until our return how long it is.

Someone has learned from a dependable source that we'll be working in a Bakelite plant. (It's not earthenware anymore?) They're supposed to have set up special tables for us in the canteen. The two gentlemen with the Lagerführer this morning came to talk with him about it.

"Hey, Kueppers Bakelite!" That name means something to us. Someone remembers having seen pictures in a magazine once: the tennis court at the Kueppers factory, the restaurant. Supposedly the serving is done by "garçons," real waiters in uniform!

"Unless they've been replaced by women because of the war. Now it's women who do the serving everywhere."

We spot the chimneys in the distance and quicken our pace. The two grandfathers, the same ones who accompanied us from the train to the camp, have a hard time keeping up with us.

"Hey . . . halt! Where are you running to, for the love of heaven?"

We stop.

"Is it much farther to the Kueppers factory?"

"But we're there!"

That's a good one!

We start walking again; the two old men at our

heels risk their breath trying to restrain us. They're clearly not joking, but what, then? We've stopped in the middle of a field.

The Kueppers factory with the tennis court, the restaurant, and the uniformed garçons, is waiting patiently—in the form of some piles of bricks and several lime kilns—to be built . . . by us. Prisoners of war (Italians) loaf among the nonexistent walls of the nonexistent factory with useless wheelbarrows and throw us friendly glances. They've certainly never heard of Papa, nor the waiters, nor the Kueppers restaurant, nor the tennis court, but we look at them with hostility, as if they were playing a joke on us. Just to provide a more appropriate setting for our distress, the sky begins to dribble.

A small consolation: If a building ever rises in that place, it will be without my help. Not that it's any fun to hang around in the rain! (On the hill you got warm at least.) But to raise so much as a little finger for these Kueppers dogs! No, thank you! I prefer dampness, rheumatism, the plague. I sit down on an overturned wheelbarrow, right in front of the foreman. Let him dare to reprimand me! He comes over and asks in Hungarian, "Are you sick?"

I don't answer. He sighs and squats beside me on the wheelbarrow.

"Can you tell me what we're doing here?"

He starts cursing. Hungarian curses are unequaled on earth, indescribable!

"How could they do that to a child!"

That was all I needed!

He shoots a grimace at the sky, which reminds me of a huge, gray, dirty beard. In his opinion, God is a sort of *Gauleiter* who creates rain, stupidity, and death.

And to think that He started with light!

Hunger, which the wet cold had driven away for a few minutes, returns ten times as strong. I swallow my saliva. For days that's all I've been doing; I'm living on my own substance. I'm devouring myself.

"Might you have something to eat?"

He frowns.

"Nothing, unfortunately."

In the meantime others have followed my example. Two Italians have joined the group. They complain about the climate.

"What will it be like in the winter!"

"In the winter! Nix winter, nix deutsch, nix war!" laughs one of the Italians, and his little monkey face, dirty and friendly, brightens.

"These macaronis, they have spirit at least!" observes the Hungarian. "But those"—he points to a cart, on improvised rails, being pushed by six men;

from a distance you can only see beards and rags—
"you never know what to expect with them. They act
like they don't know how to count to three, they
barely know two words of German, but a whole stock-
pile of explosives was recently discovered in their barracks." Russians.

A serving of dishwater is waiting for us at the camp.

Papa apologizes: a miscalculation in the kitchen.

The commandant at Plaszow, I never hated him
this much.

"The bloodsucker!" screams a hysterical voice.

"At least he doesn't gas us!"

"You call this living?"

They can barely manage to control her.

Do I have the flu? I dreamed I was already dead.
My funeral, which I attended, was quite bizarre. I saw
and heard everything, but for some unexplainable reason I didn't dare give myself away, and I reasoned:
"You're dead, be careful, they mustn't notice
you!"

—

The Lagerführer gets four marks per head per day.
Why does the Kueppers factory need our services? A
mystery. At the moment they're asking for three hundred workers. You should see the two women, the old
guards, and Papa hunting for "marks"! He spits out
obscenities unworthy of his years and his girth. The

cupboards, the toilets, under the beds—every corner is full of "deserters" (the fish business must
have been less strenuous, all things considered).
I don't have the strength to run away, and I let
myself be pushed toward the ranks, which break
apart at every moment. The show is not without savor: Papa's scarlet face, where two contrary and
equally powerful passions are struggling: (1) Whip
them to death, exterminate the whole gang; (2) Don't
lose a mark.

An autumn day, rather pleasant. We'll rest in the
fields. With some difficulty the two out-of-breath old
guards set up a chain and join it themselves, to en-
courage us; with their shaking hands they pass the
bricks. It's no use, we run away shamelessly. The
foreman, a Frenchman this time, predicts as inglorious
a future for the Kueppers factory as his Hungarian
predecessor had.

A German newspaper passes from hand to hand:
Romania has been evacuated "according to plan."
Transylvania is free. Everything is turned upside
down; the two old men are alone with the bricks,
which they continue conscientiously to stack up.

Why? That's a question no one seems to ask himself in this peculiar country. Their pitiful zeal, with
one foot in the grave. Two symbolic old men.

Transylvania is free! Is it still Hungarian? The
Frenchman doesn't know.

I notice the cart a little farther away, abandoned in the fields, halfway off its rails.

"Where are the six men?" I ask.

"I don't know," he says, taking off his hat just in case.

The road back is exhausting.

Papa greets us, looking proud and sagacious. A surprise is indeed waiting for us: a few potatoes in the soup!

—

This sneaky little fever.

I'm paying for my "luck" again.

Yesterday the departure took place with the usual ruckus. We were already lined up, some hundred and fifty of us, with no hope of getting away because the supervisors, the guards, and all the staff formed a chain around us. Meanwhile our beloved Papa was hunting for new victims. He was just in the process of pursuing Frimi from Maramures, the "brain," when the telephone in his office rang. Frimi vanished while her pursuer was talking in a dialect of which we couldn't grasp a single word. When he reappeared he was wearing a huge smile. Which, given his basic duplicity, couldn't help but worry us.

"You're free," he declared, sending the guards away.

We waited, suspicious; nobody budged.

"They telephoned from Kueppers. They don't need you today."

Too bad about his marks, we're relieved. The fugitives reappear at the windows. The paternal hand asks for silence: "The manager of the factory also told me that a property owner named Schröde needs farmhands and will give you food for the day. Since breakfast time has passed, it can only be for lunch and dinner."

He's only transmitting the message, impassive as a mailbox. He seems alarmed by the assault that follows (in which the Blockältestes and other "officials" take part).

"Was ist das?[1] Get back in ranks!"

And he starts counting. Nothing escapes his paternal vigilance; sometimes he adjusts a turban, sometimes he straightens a collar.

"Three hundred, stop," he says, and cuts the ranks right in front of my nose.

The three hundred "agricultural workers" set out toward the Schröde property, the stew, the crepes, and other marvelous things. We remain there crushed, we, the next five, who if we had only been one rank ahead . . .

They've already closed the gate, and we five are

[1] What's this?

still standing there like statues, paralyzed by our bad luck.

A hand falls on my shoulder: Papa's heavy hand covered with rings. What's he talking about? He's convulsed, his entire bulk shaking with a huge laugh.

"It was a hoax, a little joke . . ."

Tears run down his bloated, purple face. My disgust is tinged with fear: I hope he doesn't explode before he can explain.

"They've gone to Kueppers, the three hundred! The farm only asked for five people."

We, the "next five" of the decapitated column . . . We shouldn't thank him, but providence. (Providence, a funny duck!) We have to slip out discreetly. The cart is waiting for us outside. Feeding five people or three hundred isn't the same thing at all! It's up to us to make the most of the opportunity; it might amount to regular work, provided we put ourselves into it. One more word of caution: We shouldn't act too eager at the table, or throw ourselves on the food like savages. These nice people might get ideas about the camp, might imagine, for example, that we're being starved here. We all protest together: "Oh, no! What an idea!"

It's the first time that we've gone through the gate without a guard; we walk the fifty or so yards to the cart and sit down on planks behind a square back, a blond neck. Their owner doesn't turn around, doesn't say a word, waits until we're seated. We leave.

In dreams I often see myself alone in an unfamiliar street. I'm looking for my rank of five; I'm expecting to be taken back. I don't dare enjoy my solitude. Sitting in the cart, I find my "joy" clouded by similar misgivings. To cheer myself up I try not to miss anything, I greet every electric pole and every fence as if I were returning from exile or from a long illness.

The trip may have been long, but not for me; it was a time when I savored every moment.

Our vehicle stops beside a harvested field; not a sign of a house. Could this be another "hoax"? The square back jumps down on one leg. The other one is missing. He motions to us to follow him. We travel a good half mile on foot. At last we hear barking; no, it's not the Kueppers "factory"! Garden walls and chickens, and somewhere, probably, a kitchen.

A huge straw hat approaches so quickly that we can't make out the features of the person wearing it. Blond? Brunet? Young? Old? Simply in a hurry. Without a word she directs us to a field dotted with green clumps, crouches down and starts gathering potatoes and throwing them into a pail. *"Verstehen?"*[1] she asks, getting to her feet after looking at us as if it were a

---

[1] Understand?

demonstration of math or driving. I want to say that the task doesn't seem to be beyond us, but she makes a hurried gesture and vanishes before I finish my sentence. A mechanical rake goes ahead of us, dislodging the potatoes and throwing them onto the surface, white and shining. We only have to gather them up. All five of us start to work, each of us in a row. On either side are more rakes and more gatherers.

Child's play, almost a diversion. I'm out in front. Suddenly I feel a stabbing pain in my side. And from that moment everything changes. Besides the pain in my side, my back becomes an unbearable burden; to that is added the embarrassment of lagging behind, fear, and the struggle I'm waging against the temptation to straighten up just once, just for one little second—and I do!

Lots of heads turn toward me as they pass, four of them—our group—with wild looks. I crouch down again.

When I arrive at the end of my row, not too far behind, I stop. The eternity of hell that I've just been through abruptly releases me. In my dazed condition I no longer recognize the place or the people.

We're all sitting around a big table, in a big kitchen. I don't know what the dish is, steaming in the middle of the table in a pan the size of a washbasin: cabbage, mushrooms, sautéed onions, all mixed with an intoxicating odor of smoke . . . smoked sausage with rice? The lady of the house serves us first. She goes at it with a soup ladle. As I take back my plate with the fragrant pyramid piled on it, my ears buzz and I feel the blood leave my face! My hands are trembling to the point that the "pyramid" shudders and almost spills on the tablecloth. I manage to avoid the worst. But no! The worst is this woman's look. A look so heavy with pity that I carry it ever since then like a burning wound that I don't think I'll be able to forget, ever! The look you give to incurables, people worked to death, for whom nothing more can be done.

The delicious vapors go to my head. If I could be alone, just for a moment, with the steaming mound! Throw myself on it, devour it with no one watching! The first spoonfuls have almost no taste, they're so hot. I can't get over the feeling that I'm being watched. Then I don't remember any more. I must have emptied the plate in a state of trance. The woman refills it at once. This second portion I eat without haste, like a gourmet. For the first time in months I leave a plate without difficulty. Except that afterward everything goes wrong! I'm more depressed than I've ever been. As if hunger were good for something after all, and by occupying all my thoughts and all my energy it had stopped my spirits from sinking.

The "civilian" meal to which I rushed ecstatically

now sickens me, a sign of how far I've fallen! Who knows, maybe it's wiser never to fill your belly in these accursed places!

Mother! If only Sophie were with me! If the only person who took care of me hadn't gone to sleep in the railroad car! Suddenly the painful memory of my trembling hand holding the plate comes back to me, all my clumsiness . . . that burning look! I start bawling.

"Be quiet. Are you crazy?" someone whispers.

Too late.

"What is it?" murmurs the "neck."

"She's thinking about her mama."

He doesn't say anything. He pulls on the reins.

—

I've been struggling with this account for three days. I've never had such a hard time writing. It's not because of the fever, but because it's impossible to find a single position that isn't unbearable. My chest—my worst enemy—every movement, every breath stays stuck between my ribs. I'm afraid this time it's not the flu but my old acquaintance pleurisy (I had it for a whole year). To top it off, none of this affects my appetite in the slightest! The Schröde "pyramids," the aroma of cabbage, mushrooms, and I don't know what, continue to haunt me on my bed of pain.

Sarika, the scatterbrain, visits me with a plate of dishwater. This is what they call a healthy diet! And on top of everything else she starts blubbering.

"Don't worry, I'm not going to skip out! Not before I have a bacon omelet."

She leaves, annoyed, but reappears right away with a dubious character who in a weak moment passed herself off as a physician. She stands by my bedside, the very picture of indecision. (There are times when under the magical prospect of an extra ration of bread it's not hard to reincarnate yourself as a doctor, a skiing champion, a violinist, whatever.) She's gotten along fairly well until now with a few colds; she massages backs, treats migraines. But "magic" has its limits. For five minutes she tries unsuccessfully to detect my pulse. Running out of patience, I take her hand and place her index finger on the artery in question, thereby destroying what composure she had left.

"You have a fever," she declares with a woebegone look. "What does it feel like?"

"Pleurisy," I say without hesitation.

My diagnosis makes her blanch (she's only a novice fraud). She sticks her ear against my chest: "Cough!" I cough; but it's more than she can handle and she stands up, agitated: "I can't take this responsibility. I'm not equipped, I don't have medications."

"I'm going to tell the old man," says Sarika.

Protest as I may, she comes back with Papa. He bends over me with a more-than-paternal smile. Does the smoke from his cigarette bother me? No. He listens attentively to the poor "doctor" and her constant refrain: She can't take the responsibility . . . She's not a general practitioner.

"All you need to do is write the prescriptions," says Papa encouragingly, and his fox eyes glitter.

"I'm a dentist!" the poor woman groans.

"Ah!" exults the old man. "That would be nice, a *Bohrmaschine* in the camp!"

She's sweating, the "dentist." (Only an inveterate charlatan could torment a poor beginner with so much glee.)

He sends the two women away. When we're alone he tells me that in the neighboring camp just a few miles away there's a large, well-equipped dispensary, where they would get me back on my feet quickly. But what is it, why am I trembling like that? It's in my best interest, by damn!

These "very nice" dispensaries, I'm familiar with them! They've already offered me a place in one. I muster all my strength and implore him to keep me. I don't want to leave this camp no matter what.

He stares at me, puzzled.

"You'll be back in two weeks."

He seems sincere, but he's an old scoundrel, a

double-crosser! My encounter with the "ambulance" in front of the dispensary. No, I *know* what that means, a "nice" hospital! I burst into tears.

He doesn't insist, and gets ready to leave. Through my tears I continue to look at him beseechingly. He remains standing and starts interrogating me about my journal.

"Do you know that it's forbidden to take notes in the camp, that I'm risking my position, and more, by closing my eyes?"

I jump up—forgetting my ribs—and let out a groan. I mustn't worry, he isn't simply a German, he's a man first (*sic!*); he understands the importance all that could have after the war. We've suffered a lot, that's why he, for his part . . . But we mustn't forget the circumstances, with the entire country starving . . .

Nevertheless we don't lack for comforts, nor for clothes; as for the treatment, it's not even comparable to that in the concentration camps. "I'm counting on your sense of fairness . . ." He's counting on it firmly. The "bargain" he's offering is plain.

I hasten to reassure him; we'll remember him with the greatest fondness! That's why I don't want to leave this camp.

He smiles. Above the smile his eyes meet mine. In them I read anguish, and a warning: "We're done for, but watch your step—you're not out of this yet, either!"

This time he gets my broad smile. His look is more explicit than all the news that reaches us. For a second I see in it my freedom, very near, a certainty.

—

I'm in a big white hospital. From my bunk I can see a nasty, bare building, resembling a military barracks. Could it be a prisoner barracks? The striped clothes! The mud, the wind, the endless line for the soup pots, the ashen faces, the inevitable "Los, Saubande!"[1] It all reminds me of Auschwitz. Yet this is only a "subsidiary." Papa didn't lie to me; we're very close to Wiesau.

I must not be doing very well lately, because I barely had the energy to object when they loaded me onto the truck. "*Idioten*," I protested feebly, with every jolt. Even as I was saying good-bye, I almost gave in to an attack of rage when I saw the reddened eyes of Edith Berkovits and Sarika, the scatterbrain, who was bleating into her handkerchief like an old goat; what blasted right do they have to cry for me, the jerks?

The arrival is even more dramatic. I immediately

[1] Move it, you bunch of pigs!

recognize faces from Auschwitz. That's why I don't let the driver carry me in his arms. I make it up the steps and down the hall on my own two legs, and speak politely to the gawkers who look at me open-mouthed without returning my greeting. From a lack of civility, or because they're intimidated by my entourage? (They're not too used to seeing someone arrive alone, in a vehicle.)

A big surprise is waiting for me on the second floor: the woman doctor from Auschwitz, the very one who saved me from the "ambulance." (The majority of Camp B has been evacuated here.) I greet her enthusiastically, but her welcome offends me. She doesn't offer me her hand. She doesn't ask what's wrong. She immediately drags me into her office and undresses me with the help of a nurse. I haven't had time to extract my papers from the lining of my coat. I don't see my coat anymore! Decked out in "house" pajamas and bathrobe, I demand my things, panic-stricken. The nurse claims she put them away. (She doesn't look like a thief, but who isn't, when you think about it?) I try to swallow my resentment and explain the compelling reason why I have to ask for that coat. But she, the lady doctor, has her reasons, and thinks I'm getting too agitated, that my bronchia urgently need rest, etc. I'll start again tomorrow. Today I don't have the strength left. To bed! A need that

278 / ANA NOVAC

cancels out all the rest. They put pillows under my
back. My jutting bones have given me bedsores.

I fall asleep almost at once, but after a while I'm
wakened by worry.

"Where are my things?" I ask the nurse. (It's not
the one from yesterday, a fortunate creature who despite the circumstances could be called "chubby.")

"In the doctor's cupboard."

"Could you get me my green coat for a second?"

She hands it to me in secret. I'm writing all this
secretly, on toilet paper, which makes funny scribbles.
I hope to get regular paper and the strength to recopy.
Otherwise "humanity" (my sole heir) can take care of
it for me.

They want to feed me with a spoon, like a baby.
What a scream!

Can you be dying without having forebodings, and all
that? On the lower bunk one of *them* lies very quietly;
she obeys everything and says thank you for everything, with a politeness that I would never have asso-
ciated with death. But she gets little notice. I, on the
other hand, constantly get worked up and call attention to myself, in case they should forget me or start
"missing" me.

I require all sorts of medications and I make a fuss

when I have to take them. Nevertheless I think my
appetite disconcerts them. In addition to my ration, I
gobble down two more portions of soup: One is the
lady doctor's "supplement," I suppose, and the other
is what's left in the bottom of the pot.

There are black moments . . . Bah! When I look
at my hand, for example. I don't know how it happened, but it happened. It's hardly different from *her*
hand down below. But she may have given up. Or is
she refusing, too? Might every death harbor a tiger,
five minutes before? No! Sometimes I feel it slipping
toward me, the temptation: Close my eyes, let go of
this tiresome will, and all responsibility; wait for everything to be decided *elsewhere.*

Is my "tiger" made of entirely different stuff? Try
as I may to pacify it, how can I stop myself from
thinking? While I still have the strength to think, everything depends on *me* alone! As if all I have to do is
reject this "idea" . . . And every time I manage to
raise the spoon while they watch, I believe anew: I'm
the one who *decides.*

The girl below asked for something to drink. I got
down to give her something, whereupon half the ward
came running and someone called the lady doctor to
come quick.

"Who gave you permission to get out of bed?" she
asked with a calm that didn't begin to fool me.

"Why? Are you expecting the worst, by any chance?"

You should have seen their faces! Everyone took off in high gear.

In my condition, you can allow yourself certain childish behavior.

—

I've reread my latest notes: bragging.

Surprises along the way: panic, for instance.

This morning there was an unusual silence on the ward. Could there be fewer of us than yesterday? Where are the others? The woman doctor? Unfamiliar voices, whistle blasts on the stairs. I understand instantly—it's not a suspicion, or just a supposition, but certainty: They've come from Auschwitz! They're making a selection!

I want to yell . . . I change my mind because of the others. I get out of bed and fling myself pointlessly at the door. To my great surprise, it's open. I close it carefully behind me. Then I slip into the doctor's office and get my things out of the cupboard. When she arrives she finds me dressed from head to toe.

"Have you lost your mind, or what?" she asks—gently, because she isn't sure she's not making a mistake.

"I want to go to work," I say firmly.

"Listen, fifty patients don't give me as much trouble as you do all by yourself!"

"That's no reason," I say, "to let me be sent to Auschwitz."

"Get undressed," she orders.

The only reason she doesn't give me a smack is because she's too worn out. Besides, she must feel sorry for me, standing there with a resolute air, my turban on crooked, looking like a scarecrow.

"The last selection took place ten days ago, barely. They don't have railroad cars available every week." And she adds: "Don't worry, the gas doesn't work on specimens like you."

"Then why don't you give me calcium? Pleurisy is treated with calcium."

"Are you going to tell me how to prescribe the treatment now?"

She's at the end of her patience. I feel it's my last chance to play all my cards.

"You're afraid of wasting your injections! If you had the slightest hope . . ."

"I'm worried about your heart, you idiot!" she says disgustedly.

"I'll answer for my heart!"

She looks at me silently for a moment, then sighs and goes to the cupboard. I throw off my coat and wait with my arm extended.

"Sit down and make a fist!"

She tightens the tourniquet around my arm. I have to admit, I have gorgeous veins. And this time, anyway, I'm able to confirm: You can stop yourself from fainting by strength of will. Why, then, couldn't you stop yourself from dying?

In the end I don't know which of us is more exhausted. Stretched out on the couch, I don't move.

"Mind you," she says pensively, "if you get over it someday, it won't be because of the calcium."

"What, then?"

"The devil inside you."

I'm being very good. I haven't breathed a word all day. My devil is resting.

—

The girl down below has been evacuated. It was all done with the greatest discretion. The twits! Did they really think I was asleep? It seems that they're beginning to get used to the idea of my continued existence. The chubby little nurse brought me up short this morning: "No foolishness!"

When I speak to them they no longer put on that "kindly" expression. A thousand vulgarities at Auschwitz didn't exasperate me as much as the kindliness here. I hardly respond at all. What can you say to someone who has already more or less buried you!

"They'll see what they want to see," I tell myself sometimes. At other times certainty abandons me. Then I become sullen and I hate them all.

Today my neighbor—a white, flabby, bloated person who often asks me for my pencil in order to compose ballads (if only she weren't named Manette!)—this Manette, anyway, was trying to be pleasant.

"You're filling out again," she said. "My goodness!"

I grimaced. "That would surprise me. Even in 'civilian' life I looked like a prune."

"We had hair before," she mumbled. "Hair makes a big difference!"

"I used to shave my head."

She shut up. She no longer asks for my pencil. She's punishing me. I could do without it, though. I use it only rarely. The fever makes me tired. More than ever I'm resolved to hang on to life. It may be stupid and lousy, but I can't see myself without it, or it without me. Even if there were "another life," a better one, I would cling to this one, vile as it is.

—

Three days without a fever. I know that doesn't mean much. And yet. Am I kidding myself? My fingers are beginning to resemble human fingers.

—

Calcium. Silence. Emptiness.

The Russians are advancing. The Boche are pulling back! (For how many centuries?)

—

96.4.

I'm dropping toward the ice age.

—

Revierkontroll. The camp commandant and eight other people.

They line us up along the wall. Me they examine from every angle. And just when the fever has finally gone down.

Winds from Auschwitz. Shut off my brain. Don't think.

—

The lady doctor stopped by my bed today. I was too terrified to speak. I must have stared at her in an awful way, because she smiled at me and sat down on my bed.

"They've blown up two crematoriums at Auschwitz!" Her calm tone contrasted strangely with her burning eyes. "We mustn't celebrate yet; there are crematoriums at Dachau, at Buchenwald . . . God knows what they're preparing for us."

Let them prepare whatever they want to, nothing can dampen our elation. The temperature charts climb from the excitement.

—

101.1. The doctor looks at my chart with a frown. She's worried about an exudation. I don't dare tell her about my escapades. (I didn't close my eyes all night.)

It's the "muses'" fault. My neighbor, the writer of ballads, read her latest work. Everyone who could still move assembled on the upper bunks. I kept quiet, while vultures tore out the poet's heart and hyenas soaked in his blood; no end of vampires and other tortures, all of it bathed in the reader's tears and the listeners' sobs (cries and wails in places). I might have held on if it hadn't been for the surprise at the end: The poet's ashes pronouncing curses was more than I could stand, and I exclaimed, "But that's burlesque!"

It wouldn't have had any consequences! The audience didn't know the expression. The poet herself looked at me with an uncertain confidence. She would have taken it for a compliment if a hearty laugh from a lower bunk hadn't shattered all illusion.

The tear-stained faces took on aggressive expres-

286 / ANA NOVAC

sions. The author, cut to the quick, shot back coldly,
"If yours are better, come on, we're listening."
"I don't write ballads myself, but others do."
"Who?" demanded the malicious chorus, delighted
to have me cornered.
"Well, a Frenchman, for instance. Villon."
"I know," said the author, "he's from Camp B."
With a gesture she dismissed this paltry competi-
tion.
"He may have been through the camps, but not
Camp B. Ages ago he died in prison or was hanged or
something like that."
"Was he a Jew?"
"A crook, a complete scoundrel."
"Well! He wrote his poems between heists?"
They laughed.
"Why not? Nobody could stop his ballads. They've
made their author—the crook—famous throughout
the world, in every language, even Eskimo."
Did I happen to know one by heart in our lan-
guage?
"Do I know one!"
I tackled the "Ballad of the Ladies of Bygone
Times." I just murmured and watched them. The
whispers became farther apart. They seemed to like
the ballad as much as they did the preceding one,
with the blood-soaked hyenas and the ashes speaking
blasphemies.

I usually avoid "reciting," or even reading my notes out loud, not because I don't want to but because I want it too much. And that's fatal. I just have to want something madly—to dazzle people, for example—and I'll be crushed, destroyed by stage fright! That's why I don't understand how it happened; it may be that the stage fright didn't have time to catch me, that inflamed by the attention I stopped it dead. At any rate I must have slipped my moorings and set out under full sail, with feeling, gestures, the whole works. And all those eyes riveted on me, mirroring my ecstasy. I was in a trance!

Someone threw a stone. The "mirror" shattered . . .

"Who is this bag of bones?"

It wasn't meant for my ears. But can a trumpet whisper? Crestfallen faces, some of them furious, turned toward the door. Someone challenged the newcomer: "Who do you think you are, Myrna Loy?"

Don't bother! (The "bag of bones" is beyond reach.)

If it were Myrna Loy in the flesh standing at the door of the quarantine ward, I would have less trouble believing my eyes. Wearing an orange rag that clings to her thinner but still extraordinary shape, I recognize the only person I wouldn't have expected to see again in this dreary place. Yes, it's her, the "prodigy," still S-shaped—she undulates between the bunks, swinging her shopping basket, sort of like a vacationer looking for an available spot on the beach.

She finally stops beside the empty bunk below mine, throws her stuff on it, straightens up, and asks in her gruff, good-natured voice, "This is the dead girl's place, isn't it?"

We're thunderstruck.

"Yes," the chorus answers, "but how did you know?"

"I'm clairvoyant, I guess." And she adds, laughing, "That's the way it works, isn't it? Wherever you put your ass or your feet, a dead person was there before you." And then without transition: "Poor Villon, you really mistreated him, old girl!"

After the "bag of bones," this second stone only amuses me. And anyway I'm an awfully happy "bag of bones" since I saw her at the door, decked out as if for the Riviera. I ask what brings her to this place of suffering.

Nonchalantly she says, "Just typhoid fever."

A statement that makes my neighbors blanch. They retreat in disorder.

"Don't worry," she says. "Nobody has examined me. It's my own diagnosis. But where the heck have I met you?"

"At Plaszow!"

She shakes her head, looks at me, narrows her eyes, thinks.

"Didn't you live in Oradea, on Stanislo Street?"

"Yes, I did!"

"I spent the summer with your neighbors across the street, the Vas."

"I don't remember."

"You were always riding your bike."

"That's right."

"God, you were a cute kid! Are you dying, or what?"

That hits home, I'll admit! A "cute kid." As if I were now only "past tense," the relic, the wreckage of a kid. Rest her soul!

"Anyway," she says, "things aren't going any better for me. Do you remember the rump I used to have?"

She sighs so nostalgically that I can't help laughing out loud.

"And your mother?"

"You'll be shocked; she's still driving me crazy!"

Then she motions me to move over a little. I make room for her beside me.

"Listen, I'm going to attempt that ballad," she says as soon as she gets settled. "It's been on my mind for a long time."

She does it differently, I say to myself calmly. But in a few seconds my calm is only a mask.

I have a painful vision of a gesticulating skeleton, of my small voice, overwrought and pathetic. I was overdoing it, I was "acting," while she doesn't take any pains, she lets the text come alive and that's all, without any particular inflection, without "ecstasy," without gestures. The ballad rises simply from her lips, as if she were humming a melody that she loves, without thinking about it too much. At some point, I don't know when, I must have stopped thinking, too, because I don't remember any more about myself, or her—it was as if we were held suspended, or perhaps caught up in the same rhythm, borne on the same wave. "A spell!" The word came to me afterward. What's certain is that I forgot my extra helping of soup (the one I spend my days waiting for). The nurse took me by surprise when she handed me the bowl. I caught on when I heard a hoarse, excited voice beside me: "Do you still get double rations? I'm ravenous!"

I handed her the bowl, a little embarrassed not to have thought of it sooner. She took it, brought it to her lips like a bottle, and drained it in one gulp before the (flabbergasted) nurse had time to say "boo." The reaction exploded only afterward.

All these dull, thick heads! Maybe they haven't noticed that it's the salt of the earth that has deigned to descend to this forsaken spot! That when she passes by, all gloom evaporates and the desert blossoms!

God, I say to myself, dumbfounded, they'd begrudge her a miserable bowl of soup! Instead of bowing very low and humbly thanking her for being gracious enough to *exist*.

We didn't part till morning. I don't remember what we said to each other, just that it took place in a different, dizzying time. That at moments life became very strong, beyond all expressing.

Fever! Isn't it a sign of life, proof that I'm persevering, hanging on? Thank God, because after all is said and done, wouldn't it be too stupid, wouldn't it be madness, to let go of a *life* where there are such nights, and such creatures?

Epilogue

Here ends what I have managed to decipher of my journal. The last pages, like the first, are shredded. Out of seven hundred pages, that is all I was able to salvage after many months of work.

Annoying that my memory does not help me except in a sporadic and capricious way. When after such a long time (sixteen years) I made up my mind to undertake this work that I dreaded and had put off so many times, and I deciphered the lines one after another, they shocked me as if I were encountering them for the first time. "Merciful forgetfulness" banishes many events and muddles others. I'm unable to recall, for example, how long the woman doctor kept me in the hospital, or at what point we began dragging crates in the Lehmann munitions plant. (Was it there or in another factory that we were blown from one floor to another during a bombing raid?)

Was it late autumn, or was it already winter when

the march through the Alps began and for three weeks we covered twenty or twenty-five miles a day, living solely on snow and moss and running a constant risk of a bullet in the back? When did the first lice make their appearance? I don't know that either. The word "typhus" had already been on everyone's lips for a while. There were several people in the barracks who were suspect. One day a neighbor on the bunk pointed her finger at my chest and cried, "A louse?"

I looked. A little white thing, the size of a fingernail clipping.

"Is that what that is?" I asked, puzzled. "I've had them for a long time."

Our bodies, ravaged by abscesses and various infections, were tired of inventorying their ills.

I spent the last week in a munitions crate among screws and spare parts. The foreman chose the four smallest of us, risking his job to shield us from the work. When the news of the Führer's death spread, this old German, who every day gave us his own ration of milk, said these words that we found deeply puzzling: "*Und doch war er ein grosser Mann.*"[1]

———

On May 6, 1945, Soviet troops liberated the Kratzau camp. A thousand people in rags, of indeterminable

[1] And yet he was a great man!

sex, waited in front of the barracks, in the sun. They had been waiting for days.

Since the factory had closed its doors, we spent all day and all night talking about how we had lived, how we had dressed, what we had eaten in our "civilian" existence. That existence seemed so far away, almost legendary, that our own words sounded foolish, even suspicious, to us. Yet they were very simple stories: "In my bedroom, the rug was like this," or "Mama used to say that." And there we were in a fictional world, where one had *her* room, where one said the word "Mama" quite naturally.

If a stranger had heard us, he might have gotten the impression that the Nazis had torn perfectly happy people from an earthly paradise where there was neither poverty, nor stupidity, nor ugly or cruel women.

———

He's dead! We awoke to the news one morning. In front of the factory entrance we saw, on a blackboard in silver letters:

DER FÜHRER IST FÜR DEUTSCHLAND
GESTORBEN[1]

We didn't dare look at each other. But later, something happened that justified the craziest hopes:

[1] The Führer has died for Germany.

Greze, the Dragon, announced that beginning the
next day we would no longer go to work. And so
nicely! She, from whom the kindest word that I had
ever heard was: *Drecktiere.*[1] It was the end, yes, THE
END OF HIM!

—

How long did the waiting last? Years, if you judged
the time by our impatience. Actually no more than a
week went by.

The days were beautiful. Mild, warm, each one like
the others. In front of the barbed wire that separated
us from freedom, a silky lawn. A marvelous springtime
shown upon the earth, warming all hearts regardless of
race.

They arrived one afternoon. I no longer remember
who was the first to shout "There they are!"

It's always difficult to describe times of great emotion. Not only because in great joys and great sorrows
the most different people react in ways that aren't
very different, but also because the more intensely we
experience those times the less clearly we can testify
about them.

Did we shout during those first moments, or did we
wait in silence?

[1] Filth.

A column of tanks approached. Suddenly, something flew over the barbed wire: a loaf of white bread, then a second, and a third. A rain of bread.

No one moved. We stood rooted, whiter than the loaves of bread falling from the sky. Before our eyes lay a sea of vehicles covered with dust. And as if emerging from a gigantic cloud, hundreds of faces.

A lone soldier came through the gate. He stopped for a moment and looked at us without a word. In the bright sunshine, the sight that we presented must not have been very reassuring.

"Isn't there a girl here from Odessa? Vera Jutkovitz?" he asked in Yiddish.

Glossary

actions*	mass killings
Appelplatz*	square where the prisoners were lined up in formation to be counted ("roll call")
Bergkapo*	Kapo supervising the work on the hill
Bergkommando*	SS squad leader
Blockälteste*	head of the barracks
Blocksperre*	barracks curfew
Blokowa*	(female) head of the barracks, in Polish
Boche	disparaging term for a German, dating from World War I
Bohrmaschine	drill
Charlotte Corday	woman who assassinated Marat in his bath, during the French Revolution
Csongor and Tünde	a classic children's play
Die Vögelein im Walde	"The little birds in the woods"
Duce	"il Duce" (the leader), Benito Mussolini
Faust	play by Johann von Goethe
Fritz	slang term for German soldier

*Camp term

Gauleiter	Nazi regional official
Idioten	idiots
Kapo*	prisoner foreman of a labor squad
Lagerälteste*	head prisoner of the camp
Lagerführer*	SS officer in charge of the camp
Lagerkapo*	high-ranking Kapo
Lagersperre*	camp curfew
Lagerstrasse*	camp street
Maramures	a "county" in Transylvania; one of forty administrative divisions of Romania
Miskolc	a town in Hungary
Oradea	a town in Romania, near the Hungarian border
O tempora!	from Latin O Tempora! O Mores! (O Times! O Customs!)
Revierkontroll	hospital inspection
Schwerverbrecher	premeditated murderer
Sonderkommando*	work squad (gas chamber and crematorium)
Stubendienst*	detainee in charge of food or housekeeping
Szenttamas	a town in Hungary
transport*	convoy of prisoners
Waschraum*	disinfection hall
Zählappel*	roll call of the prisoners
Zarathustra	Thus Spake Zarathustra (Nietzsche)

*Camp term

Notes

Ana's diary is one of the few records to survive from the camps. Several Sonderkommandos at Auschwitz wrote and buried accounts of their activities. Their manuscripts were recovered in the area of the crematoria. The first notebooks were found in March 1945, buried near crematorium #3 in a tin mess kit; in 1952, a diary was uncovered near crematorium #2; another document on July 28, 1961; and another in a glass jar, near crematorium #3, was found on October 17, 1962. It is very likely that there were more documents to be retrieved and that many or most of them were destroyed by moisture, animals, and time or, after liberation, by Poles digging for the gold they believed the Jews had brought to Auschwitz. The source of the history and contents of these manuscripts as well as discussions of the Jewish resistance movement is Ber Mark's *The Scrolls of Auschwitz*, (Tel Aviv: Oved Publishers Ltd., 1985).

Second, included in a poetry anthology, *Against Forgetting: Twentieth-Century Poetry of Witness*, edited by Carolyn Forche (New York: Norton, 1993), are poems by Miklos Radnoti written from August to October 1944 in forced labor camps and on a death march; these poems were found in his pockets when his body was exhumed in 1946. Along with twenty other men on a death march, he was shot in early November 1944 by Hungarian non-commissioned officers.

Third, in *Bearing the Unbearable: Yiddish and Polish Poetry in the Ghettos and Concentration Camps*, Frieda W. Aaron includes poetry by Jozef Bau, written in Gross-Rosen and Plaszow (Albany, NY: SUNY Press, 1990).

Finally, the drawings, paintings, and poems by children and adults at Theresienstadt also constitute documentation from a Nazi camp. Undoubtedly, at least a few more manuscripts written in the Nazi camps will come to light.

Page 6: In the middle of her journal, Novac tells the story of her arrest on a train from Miskolc, where she had been enrolled in a Jewish high school for girls, to Oradea, where she was supposed to meet her parents. She was arrested in May, 1944. Although the majority of both houses of the Hungarian Parliament had passed anti-Semitic laws as early as May 28, 1938, it wasn't until March 19, 1944, that the Nazis occupied Hungary. By April 5, 1944, Hungarian Jews were required to wear a yellow star. Deportations to Auschwitz started on May 15 and continued through October.

In early May, the Jews of Northern Transylvania, the district in which Novac's hometown Oradea was located, were placed in ghettos. Oradea had the second largest Jewish population in Hungary, with over twenty-one thousand Jews in 1941. The ghetto in Oradea was full by May 9, so the Nazis established a smaller ghetto in the city, near the Mezey lumberyard. Novac was probably deported from this site on one of the transports that arrived in Auschwitz between May 24 and 31, where she would have been admitted as a "depot prisoner," that is, a prisoner who was neither gassed on arrival nor registered but kept in quarantine. Novac begins her story while she is in quarantine in Auschwitz-Birkenau.

Page 17: This journal opens with the infamous *Zählappel*, or roll call. The Nazis held roll call twice a day, before dawn and at dusk, after the twelve- to fourteen-hour workday, in every kind of weather. The roll calls usually lasted from two to five hours but were frequently twenty-four hour ordeals. Every prisoner, dead or alive, had to be accounted for. Virtually all Holocaust memoirists describe these grueling and cruel events, many of which were *strafappel*, or punishment roll calls. The SS officers also required the prisoners to witness torture and hangings during roll call. As Novac puts it, "You made your will before every roll call."

In recalling the way the prisoners managed to retain their dignity and self-control during these unbearable circumstances, Lucie Adelsberger says, "Roll call was not the only horror of the day; it was also a revelation as to how human beings can rise above themselves." (*Auschwitz: A Doctor's Story.* Boston: Northeastern University Press, 1995, p. 50).

Page 16: Auschwitz itself, the largest concentration camp in the Third Reich, covered about twenty-five square miles and has become known as the "largest graveyard in human history." It was divided into three parts: Auschwitz I, a concentration/death camp of about thirty two-story brick barracks, a small gas chamber, and the site of inhuman medical experiments and torture; Auschwitz II, or Birkenau, a massive complex of about three hundred barracks and four enormous gas chambers; and Auschwitz III, a group of forced labor industrial sites to which the SS sent Jews and other prisoners. The industries paid the SS a small sum per day for each "slave." In June 1940, the first camp commandant, SS Capt. Karl Fritzch, announced to a group of newly arrived prisoners: "You have not come to a sanitarium but to a German concentration camp and the only way out is through the chimney of the crematorium. If there's anybody who doesn't like it, he can walk into the wire right away. If there are any Jews in a transport, they have no right to live longer than two weeks, priests for a month, and the rest for three months." The name *Auschwitz* has become the symbol for the most cruel and barbarous conditions one can imagine.

Auschwitz-Birkenau was divided into nine contiguous sub-camps, each separated by double rows of electrified barbed wire. The sub-camps were designated as camps BIa and BIb (both women's camps), BIIa (men's quarantine camp), BIIb (family camp from Theresienstadt), BIIc (Hungarian women's camp), BIId (men's main camp), BIIe (Gypsy camp), BIIf (prisoners' hospital), and BIII (unfinished section of camp, called "Mexico," which was liquidated on October 6, its prisoners sent to BIIc).

Page 21: Novac is describing a selection, the process by which an SS officer, almost always a physician, glances at rather than examines the parade of naked bodies to determine who looks sickly and unable to endure forced labor. Those selected will be sent to the gas chambers. Selections were unannounced and, of course, dreaded. Novac describes selections throughout the journal. See, especially, the one in which she and Sophie volunteer to go to an "easier" camp, but Hella pulls them back because she knows that the Nazis will send the volunteers, the girls under sixteen, to the gas chamber.

Page 24: Hella is probably a Kapo, a prisoner appointed by the SS to be the head of a work group, or a block (barracks) elder, an SS-appointed prisoner responsible for the cleanliness of the barracks. They carried sticks or whips or some other instrument with which to hit the prisoners.

In return for helping the Nazis enforce the rules and run the camp, Kapos and other privileged prisoners were given more food and better conditions and thus had a better chance to survive than the other prisoners.

Page 29: The "bunks" were slatted wooden roosts about three feet by six feet, on which six women slept. Three tiers of these bare wood shelves actually made up a bunk. In turn, three rows of the bunks ran down the length of the barracks. The width of the aisles between them was about eighteen inches.

Page 30: The Final Solution is the official term the Germans used to denote the extermination of Europe's Jews.

Page 31: The Nazis constructed a double row of electrified barbed wires to deter escapes, but prisoners who gave up their will to live sometimes "went to the wire" in order to die. Official Auschwitz Order # 17/44, of June 9, 1944, states that the barbed wire fences had to be electrified twenty-four hours a day because the Hungarian Jews repeatedly fled the crematorium buildings in an effort to escape. Apparently, there had been periods when the "fences" were electrified only at night.

Page 33: The Russians didn't reach Auschwitz until January 27, 1945.

Page 34: After three weeks of quarantine in Auschwitz, Ana's group was transported to Plaszow, a concentration camp in the suburbs of Cracow but within the city limits on the site of two Jewish cemeteries. It was enlarged several times to accommodate Polish and Jewish prisoners. In May and June, 1944, transports of about eight thousand Hungarian Jews brought the total number of prisoners to about twenty-five thousand. Jewish prisoners were separated from Poles and others and were starved, beaten, shot, or worked to death. Disease took its toll, too.

Page 52: The Germans bombed Cracow on September 1, 1939, and occupied the city on September 6.

Page 53: The hill was the site of official shootings, but the Jewish Kapo (whom Novac describes in detail throughout her journal) beat prisoners anywhere in the camp and Commandant Goeth shot prisoners randomly, according to many, many eyewitnesses, everywhere in the camp.

Page 56: The camp commandant at this time was Amon Goeth, universally acknowledged as a sadist. He headed Plaszow from February 11, 1943 to September 13, 1944, when the Germans arrested him for stealing from the Reich, that is, taking the prisoners' valuables. Never brought to trial by the Germans, he was tried in August and September, 1946, by the Allies on charges that he caused the death of about eight thousand prisoners of Plaszow and liquidated both Cracow and Tarnow ghettos, thereby causing the death of thousands more. He was also charged with "wholesale murder." Goeth pleaded not guilty. The tribunal found him guilty and sentenced him to death. He was executed in Cracow.

Two Jewish women who were adults during their incarceration in Plaszow wrote graphic and horrifying portrayals of Amon Goeth, corroborating trial records as well as the book and film *Schindler's List:* Bertha Ferderber-Salz, *And the Sun Kept Shining* (New York: Holocaust Library, 1980) and Malvina Graf, *The Krakow Ghetto and the Plaszow Camp Remembered* (Tallahassee: Florida State University Press, 1989).

Page 60: The Russians liberated Cracow on January 18, 1945.

Page 113: The failed attempt on Hitler's life took place on July 20, 1944. The high-ranking German officers who plotted to kill him were discovered and tortured to death.

Page 185: Madame Potrez died on the day that Kommandant Goeth was arrested, September 13, 1944. His successor was equally brutal.

Page 186: Danuta Czech's *Auschwitz Chronicle* (New York: Henry Holt, 1990) indicates that a group of two thousand Jewish women from Plaszow arrived on October 22, 1944. On the next day, the notorious Dr. Mengele conducted a selection and sent 1,765 women to camp BIIc. In all probability, this transport was the last to leave Plaszow before the camp was liquidated. Novac may have been transported earlier and the transport may not have been noted in the Auschwitz records. Because she wrote about Goeth's arrest, she was clearly in the camp in mid-September.

Page 189: The women say that their transport was huge—about ten thousand—but were misled or confused.

Page 200: Ella refers to the Czech (or Theresienstadt) family camp, which was composed of transports of about five thousand Jews each.

This camp was unique because the Nazis did not separate them by age or sex, allowed them to keep their luggage, provided better food and a school for the children, presumably staged to deceive an anticipated visit from a Red Cross team, which never took place. The Jews were quarantined in camp BIIb for six months and gassed on March 7, 1944. The camp authorities gave each subsequent transport of Jews from Theresienstadt exactly six months to live.

Page 201: Tattooing began in March 1942, and 405,000 prisoners were given numbers. The Nazis did not "process" and tattoo the hundreds of thousands of Jews whom they sent to the gas chambers directly from the trains.

Page 213: The women from Rhodes suffered an extraordinary ordeal. Their transport left Rhodes on July 24, 1944, and reached Auschwitz on August 16, where they stayed for two and one half months before being shipped to a series of labor camps in Germany. Besides the deplorable conditions, the Rhodians faced extreme hardship because of the difference in climate from their native land and their unfamiliarity with the languages spoken in the camps. Of the original 2,500 deportees, 346 men and 254 women were registered in the camp; the rest were sent to the gas chambers on arrival.

Page 235: The Allies' unresponsiveness to Jewish requests to bomb Auschwitz and its railroad lines is still the topic of much controversy. However, on September 13, 1944, the Americans bombed synthetic oil plants at Odertal and Monowitz (Auschwitz III) and, by mistake, bombed Auschwitz I and hit an SS barracks. SS casualties numbered fifteen dead and twenty-eight injured. Twenty-three Jews working in the clothing workshop were also killed. In the same raid, the Americans dropped bombs on Birkenau (Auschwitz II), damaging the railroad line leading into the camp. David S. Wyman reports that from July to December, air strikes over the synthetic oil production factories were extensive and intensive, but no attempt was made to bomb and thereby halt the killing operation (see "Why Auschwitz Wasn't Bombed," in Michael Berenbaum and Yisrael Gutman, *Anatomy of the Auschwitz Death Camp.* Bloomington and Washington, D.C.: Indiana University Press and the United States Holocaust Memorial Museum, 1994, 569–87). Martin Gilbert provides a similar analysis from the British perspective in "The Question of Bombing Auschwitz," in *The Nazi Concentration Camps: Pro-*

ceedings of the Fourth Yad Vashem International Historical Conference. Jerusalem: Yad Vashem, 1984, 417–73.

If Novac was transported to Auschwitz before October 22, she may be referring to the September 13 raid and, through the rumor mill, she may have received inaccurate information about the casualties. If, however, she did arrive on the October transport, she is probably referring to one of the later air raids on the oil plants.

Page 240: Dr. Josef Mengele experimented on twins, ages two to adult, selecting them from the transports as well as from the Gypsy and the Czech family camps. Twins were not assigned work; they were exclusively Mengele's. They were measured, examined, X-rayed, and photographed. Experiments included blood transfusions, vivisections, injections of chemical substances, surgical procedures (including sewing twins together), and eye-color research. Estimates vary, but it is generally agreed that he performed his experiments on about eight hundred twins. Prisoner doctors were assigned to assist him.

Page 259: The Kueppers factory was a munitions plant located in Wiesau, Lower Silesia, Poland. According to prisoner testimony, it opened in September 1944 and its last mention is January 1945. This would mean that Ana was transferred out of Plaszow in mid-September at the latest (but she had to have been there on September 13 because she refers to events that happened that day) and out of Auschwitz very soon after she arrived. On the other hand, it is very likely that prisoner testimony about the first mention of Kueppers is slightly off.

Page 284: According to Auschwitz records, the prisoner resistance movement staged an uprising on October 7, 1944, and blew up Crematorium IV. Fighting broke out at Crematoria II and III. The Crematorium IV Sonderkommando (those prisoners selected by the SS who worked in the gas chambers and crematoria) escaped to the adjacent woods but were killed or captured. Seven hundred and fifty Sonderkommandos were killed, and 663 survived the revolt. Several hundred were shot that evening. Three SS died in the uprising.

On November 25, the Berlin Headquarters issued orders to destroy the crematoria. Wrecking crews began work on Crematorium III on December 1. On January 26, the day before the Soviets liberated Auschwitz, an SS squad destroyed Crematorium V.

Index

(Page numbers in *italics* refer to illustrations.)